The Inner Coach

by **Dave Power**

with Dorothy Sheehy-Wieczorek

Bloomington, IN

author**HOUSE**®

Milton Keynes, UK

AuthorHouse™
1663 Liberty Drive, Suite 200
Bloomington, IN 47403
www.authorhouse.com
Phone: 1-800-839-8640

First published by AuthorHouse 8/7/2007

ISBN: 978-1-4343-1940-1 (sc)

Printed in the United States of America
Bloomington, Indiana

This book is printed on acid-free paper.

Special thanks to Dorothy Sheehy-Wieczorek whose skillful writing transformed my written material into concise and cohesive chapters. I am deeply grateful for her dedication and contributions throughout the process of writing this book and for making my lifelong dream become a reality.

Acknowledgments

This book is the culmination of the efforts of many dedicated people. I would like to especially thank...

Brad Wolverton for his ideas, advice, and for his skillful writing of the introduction, epilogue and for editing the chapters;

Fran Conn for her keen eye for both editorial and design detail;

Al Johnson for providing the photographs for the front and back covers;

My high school coach, Keith Andersen and college coach, Bill Landin, who were most influential in the development of my game;

All my former high school and college teammates who challenged me during endless hours of practice to be the best I could be;

All my colleagues and professional staff for their feedback.

To my
beautiful wife and best friend Eileen
for her love and continuous support of me
and my professional endeavors

In memory
of my parents and biggest fans,
Mildred and John Power,
for their loving support on and off the court.

Chapter Overview

Introduction

IN ONE OF THE BIGGEST MATCHES OF MY LIFE, I PLAYED ARTHUR ASHE during the summer of 1965 on the grass courts of the International Tennis Hall of Fame in Newport, R.I. I was 20, and coming off an All-American year at Indiana University, and Arthur, a future teammate of mine on the U.S. traveling team, had just won the NCAA singles and doubles championships for UCLA.

Grass was one of my favorite surfaces, and entering the match I was brimming with confidence. During the summer circuit, I had scored big singles wins over several fellow All-Americans and had won doubles events in Cincinnati and Detroit. But matching up against Arthur, who was fast becoming one of the world's top players, would give me a chance to test my talents against another level of player. With a win against him, I could serve notice that I too was a player on the international stage.

I dropped the first set, 8-6. But knowing that I was holding my own against such a top player, I opened the second set full of confidence. Word was starting to spread around the grounds that Arthur was in a tight match, and a crowd had gathered around the court.

We stayed on serve through the first 14 games of the second set until I got my first break point—a set point—at 8-7. Here I was with a chance to take a set against a guy who would reach the Australian Open final a mere five months later. What could be better?

At 30-40, my mind raced. I planned out exactly what I wanted to do depending on where I thought he might serve. He had been serving and volleying the whole match, so I assumed he would come in even at such a tight moment. I decided if he served to my backhand, I would hit my slice crosscourt doubles return, forcing him to volley a low backhand. I assumed that he would hit his first volley down the line, the highest percentage shot, allowing me to hit one of my favorite shots—my running crosscourt pass.

I bounced on my toes and leaned forward, ready to pounce. Just as I had expected, Arthur sliced his serve to my backhand. I hit my return perfectly, low and tight over the net to his backhand, just as planned. He approached the net and hit a low, backhand volley down the line—again, just as expected. I had to hurry, but I knew I had a play on the ball. I zeroed in on it as I ran across the grass and lined up what I hoped would be my winning passing shot. I was hitting my favorite shot, and felt relaxed and confident.

Swooooosh!

I couldn't believe it—I had completely missed the ball! The combination of the grass and underspin Arthur had put on the ball caused the ball to skid under my racquet and never come up. I couldn't let the bad luck get me down. I needed to compose myself for the next point.

Unfortunately, Arthur held serve, and at 9-9 the match was suspended because of darkness. The next day we resumed play and both held serve a few more times. He eventually won the set 13-11.

Twenty years later I was reading Arthur's autobiography and was amazed to read that he considered his low backhand volley to be one of his best shots. Here I thought I had the best plan for that point, and instead I played right into his strength.

Arthur went on to win three majors…the U.S. Open, Australian Open, and Wimbledon, and become one of the most celebrated athletes of any generation because of his humanitarian work. Although I competed well the next two years, reaching the round of 32 at the U.S. Nationals at Forest Hills and winning one singles event, I never had enough big weapons to become a Top 10 player in the world. But what allowed me to compete against world-class competition was my ability to play smart tennis at crucial moments and coach myself through matches.

After I stopped competing, I turned my attention to teaching the game, passing along those self-coaching techniques to help other players identify and correct their errors. During more than 35 years as a high-school coach, a Division I men's and women's college coach, and directing tennis academies at several clubs including the Windward Lake Club, in Alpharetta, Ga., I have been fortunate to work with players who won five national championships, two who went on to reach the world Top 50, and countless other nationally ranked players.

Over the years, grips and strokes have evolved—but the mental side of the game has not really changed. Players spend countless hours honing proper stroke technique and footwork, but to reach the top levels of the game they must develop a good mental foundation. I wrote this book to help competitive players of all ages learn more about the mental side of tennis, to aid high school coaches and teaching professionals, as well as parents preparing junior players for the intricacies of the mental game.

The mental side of tennis is one of the more difficult aspects of the game to understand, but it is my hope that the tips and tools this book provides will help make that part of the game easier to master. I suggest you read it in small doses, as there is a lot to grasp. Take one chapter at a time and work on the strategies and tactics during your practice matches until they become natural.

Then think of the book as a reference tool that you should refer to continually during your career. With this approach, you will gradually improve your mental game until you master all the concepts and become a smarter player.

1

Philosophy of Match Play

EVERY COMPETITIVE TENNIS PLAYER MUST DEVELOP A BASIC PHILOSOPHY that will guide his approach to each and every match. This philosophy, or set of guiding beliefs, will provide a mental framework he will utilize in making important choices on the court. Together with these beliefs, the player must also develop specific goals that will help him establish a successful game plan. By combining a strong basic philosophy with realistic match goals (covered in Chapter 3), he will build a solid foundation for a tough mental game. *This strong basic philosophy needs to begin with a belief in himself.*

There are eight essential beliefs a player must have for a winning mental game and they are the following:

I WILL STAY POSITIVE

The player must expect to win the match. Even if his opponent's ability is greater, a mentally prepared player realizes there are many factors that can equalize a match and affect the outcome. For instance, his opponent might not play up to his ability level that day for several reasons: he might be injured or recovering from an illness; he might not play well in wind or poor weather conditions; he might develop cramps on hot days; or, he might choke at a critical time in the match. The player must be *positive* in his belief that he can win. *If he enters the match with a negative attitude, he will find a way to lose it.* In many matches, both players will have opportunities to win. In close matches, the win will go to the player whose belief in winning is strongest.

I WILL NEVER GIVE UP

The player who never gives up is very difficult to beat because *he is always mentally in the match*, regardless of the score. He has the ability to turn a match around and frequently makes tremendous comebacks because he knows the match is not over until he loses match point. Even if he is playing poorly, the player still possesses the ability to compete. When frustrated or discouraged, many players either do not make the necessary comeback, or they begin the comeback too late. Tanking, or giving up before the match is over, can be viewed as the opposite of this principle. One who tanks a match is a negative thinker who would prefer not to try, rather than give the appearance of trying and losing. Tanking is a losing philosophy that reflects poorly on the player involved.

I WILL WIN UGLY IF NECESSARY

The player must find a way to win in any manner possible within the rules. This might mean hitting thirty balls per point and playing for three hours, or taking some pace off a hard-hit ball. The baseliner may need to come to the net, or the serve-and-volley player may need to stay back and rally. It is acceptable to win ugly, because looking good isn't as important as winning. It is not essential to stroke every ball. Sometimes, a defensive block of the ball is the more effective way to handle a deep, hard-hit shot.

I WILL NEVER ALTER A WINNING STRATEGY

There is no reason to change a winning game. The player is winning because he is playing the right game against his opponent. If his opponent changes his strategy, then he may have to counter with some changes of his own. The player who changes a winning game without reason often creates a more difficult situation for himself. He may even lose a match that he had control over. This approach is especially important to remember toward the end of a set when there is more pressure on each shot. Under pressure, many players who are winning change their strategy for no apparent reason. Instead, remember that it is always mentally smart to stay with what is working well.

I WILL ALWAYS CHANGE A LOSING GAME

If a player is losing badly, then he obviously needs to make a change. First, he must determine why he is losing, and then he must make the proper adjustments. If that does not work, the player needs to change his game. He might even win the match with a very different style of play than he had originally intended. Staying with a losing game will never lead to victory. (Chapter 3 will provide tips about how to change a losing game.)

I WILL WIN MOST POINTS ON ERRORS NOT WINNERS

Smart players will focus on forcing their opponents into errors rather than hitting their own winning shots. Many points are lost in a match because the player overhits the ball. A winner might look good and feel good to him, but the effort in trying to hit a winner adds unnecessary pressure to the shot. The smart player knows that it is impossible to hit winners continuously. He knows he must be patient until he has the right opportunity to attempt a winner.

It is important to focus more on hitting *winning shots* rather than *winners*. Make an opponent hit a wide ball on the run, or a ball below the net when he is volleying. Relying on these shots will help a player win most of his points off his opponent's errors.

I WILL PLAY HIGH-PERCENTAGE SHOTS

One of the most common mistakes made during match play occurs when the player tries to hit a better shot than what is needed for the situation. Which is worse: Keeping the ball in play and losing the point, or going for too much and losing the point? It's always better for a player to keep balls in play.

It is essential to note that this principle does not advocate the concept of "playing not to lose." Although the player should strive to keep the ball in play, he does not want to play so conservatively that he is giving his opponent a better chance to win than himself. Keeping the ball in play with some aggressiveness is playing to win. The smart player wants to hit the ball well enough to force his opponent into making an error, while at the same time taking as little risk as possible in hitting that shot. The player's ability to do this is one of the determining factors in how high a level of play he will achieve.

I KNOW MY OPPONENT CAN MISS ANY SHOT...AT ANY TIME

Remember, there are no easy shots in tennis. Even though some shots may be easier to handle than others, there is always the possibility that an opponent might miss any particular shot. Even professional players miss easy shots once in a while. The more pressure there is during a certain moment in a match, the greater the chance an opponent might miss. The player who is aware that his opponent can miss any shot at any time will realize the importance of keeping the ball in play and winning points through unforced errors. (Chapter 4 will deal with ways a player can learn how to concentrate more effectively to avoid missing such easy shots.)

2

Analyzing An Opponent's Game

IN EVERY MATCH, A PLAYER NEEDS TO ASSESS HIS OPPONENT'S STRENGTHS and weaknesses as quickly as possible. His analysis will guide his shot selection and point development during the match. His assessment begins in the warm-up as he analyzes the consistency of each stroke and selects certain shots to see how well his opponent handles them. Because it's not possible to analyze his opponent's entire game during the warm-up, he continues to pay strict attention to each shot during the first few games to further determine his opponent's strengths and weaknesses. He will have an advantage in the match if he can detect shots his opponent does not like or does not have.

GROUNDSTROKES

Assess both the opponent's forehand and backhand by hitting the following shots:

- ▸▸ A ball hit directly at him to see whether he chooses to take the shot with a forehand or a backhand
- ▸▸ A short underspin shot to see how smoothly he handles it and to get a look at how well he hits his approach shot
- ▸▸ A fast-paced shot to see how well he handles pace
- ▸▸ A slow ball to assess the opponent's timing for that pace and how well he generates his own pace
- ▸▸ A topspin shot that bounces at least up to his shoulders to assess how strong he is and how well he handles this high bounce

▸▸ A wide ball which causes his opponent to hit late and on the run. This will evaluate his movement, footwork and racquet preparation

▸▸ Several different angled shots to see if they create errors.

SERVE

It is important for him to ask himself:

▸▸ How fast is the opponent's first serve? This will dictate how much backswing to use on the return. The faster his serve, the shorter the backswing.

▸▸ What type of spin does he use for his first and second serves?

▸▸ How close to the service line does his serve land? Can he hit first and second serves to both corners well?

▸▸ What is his most effective serve?

▸▸ Can his toss be read as to which serve is coming and to what location?

▸▸ Can the second serve be attacked?

The smart player will practice his serve before the warm-up so he has time to return some of his opponent's serves. These practice returns will prepare his timing for the first return game.

The information gathered in the warm-up is a starting point and the accuracy of that assessment will need to be verified in the first few games. The following strokes may or may not be able to be analyzed in the warm-up. The player will want to assess them as soon as possible once the match begins.

VOLLEY

▸▸ Are his hands strong and quick enough to handle pace?

▸▸ Can he handle a ball hit directly at him?

▸▸ Does he have trouble timing and controlling a ball hit shoulder-high or higher?

▸▸ Can he handle a low volley?

▸▸ How successfully does he volley when leaning or stretching for the ball?

▸▸ How well does he execute a half volley?

▸▸ Does he have trouble handling a slower ball and can he generate his own pace off it?

OVERHEAD

▸▸ How confidently does he attack the ball?

▸▸ How well can he hit his overhead from behind the service line?

▸▸ How well does he run down a lob hit well over his head?

▸▸ How successful is he hitting an overhead on his backhand side?

The player combines this information on the volley and overhead to predict how often his opponent might come to the net, and also how good his own passing shots and lobs will need to be if he is to be successful.

LOB

▸▸ Is it well disguised?

▸▸ How well does he hit it on the run?

▸▸ Can he hit both topspin and underspin lobs?

▸▸ Does he lob well off balls hit below his knees?

▸▸ Does he lob better off a fast or slow paced ball?

The opponent who consistently lobs well plays good defense and has good hands. He can discourage the player from coming to the net. The player will have to make sure he chooses the right shot when he approaches the net.

SERVICE RETURN

▸▸ Which serve does he have the most trouble with: Flat or spin? High or low bounce?

▸▸ Does he hit the return better when the serve is hit close to the body or when reaching out wide?

▸▸ How well does he handle the serve hit directly at him?

This analysis becomes critical when serving big points. It will dictate the right serve to use to help win the point.

APPROACH SHOT

▸▸ Which side does he hit the better approach shot from— forehand or backhand?

▸▸ Does he always hit his approach shot deep down the line?

▸▸ Can he routinely hit a winner off the short ball?

▸▸ Does he have difficulty hitting approach shots from any particular height?

The player needs to assess how difficult it will be to hit a lob or a passing shot off his opponent's approach. The better the approach shot, the more important it will be for him to keep his shots deep.

PASSING SHOTS

▸▸ Which passing shot is hit harder and/or more accurately: Down-the-line or cross-court? Forehand or backhand?

▸▸ Can he hit a short-angled crosscourt shot?

▸▸ Is he able to make the ball dip below the net to make the volley more difficult?

The backhand down-the-line passing shot is typically the weakest shot for most players. Find out if the opponent can hit this shot, and if so, how effectively.

DROP SHOT

▸▸ Can his shot be read?

▸▸ Which side does he prefer hitting it from?

▸▸ What ball pace does he prefer to use for the shot?

▸▸ At what height does he prefer to hit it from?

▸▸ Is he always inside the baseline when he hits it?

A well-disguised drop shot is difficult to read and very effective, even at the highest levels of the professional game. Therefore, the player needs the answers to these questions in order to anticipate the situations when his opponent is most likely to use it.

The smart player uses the information in this chapter to analyze and determine his opponent's strengths and weaknesses. The answer to a particular question may change over the course of a match, as not all opponents give away their strengths and weaknesses during a warm-up session. Using these questions regularly, he will help develop a smart game plan and give himself a good idea of what to expect in each match he plays.

3

Mastering the Three Battles

THERE ARE THREE DISTINCT BATTLES THAT OCCUR SIMULTANEOUSLY DURING every match. They pertain to the match strategy, the emotional state of mind, and the physical endurance of each player. Although a smart player understands that the three battles are interrelated, he will have specific goals for dealing with each of them. The sooner a player begins working on winning these battles during a match, the more success he will have in dictating play and ultimately in winning the match. *The capability of his opponent to compete will decrease each time the player attains his goal for one of the battles.* Many times, the edge in a match will go to the player who is the tougher competitor mentally and who dominates the three ongoing battles of the match.

BATTLE #1: DEVELOPING A WINNING STRATEGY

Every player has individual strengths and weaknesses that determine the best strategies for him to employ during matches. A player must begin the match with a game plan of how he intends to win. *His goal is to expose and exploit his opponent's weaknesses and to negate his opponent's strengths.* If the player is a baseliner, he must be content to stay back and play long rallies to win his points. His weapons are solid groundstrokes and a good return of serve. The baseliner uses precise placements and steadiness to force errors. On the other hand, if the player is a net rusher, he will want to get to the net as quickly as possible to finish points. His weapons will include a big serve, a strong volley, and a good overhead. The net rusher's game plan is to serve and volley and come to the net off his groundstrokes or return of serve so that he might take full advantage of his weapons. The all-court player is confident playing either from the baseline or the net. He will have to decide which of the above styles or a combination is best suited to defeat his opponent. His versatility provides him the most options in his game plan. In order to be effective in this first battle, the player must strive to establish his game before his opponent gains control with his strategy.

During the first four or five games the player must pay attention to both his game and his opponent's game. He needs to understand what is working and how he is winning most of his points. He needs to recognize the errors his opponent makes, especially unforced errors. He should hit the same shots again to see if he solicits another error. If his opponent makes the same error, he may have found a weakness. He can then choose to exploit the weakness repeatedly throughout the match or just occasionally when he finds himself needing a critical point.

WHEN TO CHANGE THINGS UP

If the player is losing more than 50% of his points or has lost three games in a row, he must ask himself, "Am I getting beat?" or "Am I beating myself?" The smart player will figure out why he is losing and will make the proper adjustments. If the player is beating himself, *he must focus on playing longer points and make steadiness a higher priority than winning points.* He will need to increase his concentration on the margin he is using, aim for fewer lines and play more consistent shots.

GETTING BEAT

Whenever the player is losing, he must evaluate if he is making it easier for his opponent to beat him by the type of shots he is hitting. He must ask himself:

▶▶ Am I hitting every ball at my opponent's favorite pace?

▶▶ Are my shots landing short or down the middle?

▶▶ Can I change my shot placement and be more effective?

▶▶ Am I using all my shot options against my opponent?

Once he recognizes the problem, he can make the proper adjustments to win more points. If he is still losing games after making these adjustments and also playing more consistently, then it is time to consider a change in strategy. If the player senses the match is slipping away with the way he is presently playing, he must alter his game plan while he still has time to turn the match around. The change needs to begin no later than the first few games of the second set after losing the first set. (This same necessity to alter his game plan may occur at the start of the third set after losing the second set).

HOW TO ALTER STRATEGIES

The losing baseline player will have to come to the net more often and force his opponent to stay back and hit passing shots from the baseline. He can accomplish this by serving and volleying, returning and coming to the net, or approaching the net during a baseline rally. If he is losing to a baseliner, he can take his opponent out of his comfort zone by bringing him to the net with short balls and drop shots.

The losing net player can change shot placement before he abandons the net for the baseline (see Chapter 8 on Match Tactics). If these changes do not produce results, he must play more from the baseline and attack only at good opportunities.

WINNING FIRST SET, LOSING SECOND

The player must analyze why he lost the second set. He may have changed a winning game, become less aggressive and allowed his opponent to dictate points. He must return to hitting the type of shots he was using while winning. Or, perhaps his opponent changed his game and the player failed to recognize it. He must reverse this trend, become more aggressive and change the momentum of the match.

The proper adjustments will make it more difficult for his opponent to continue winning. The player will realize he is on the right track if the momentum begins to shift and the match starts to turn around. *He may win the match with a style of play that is totally different from the style with which he started.* The smart player knows it is essential to try every possible tactic to win a match. Both the timing of the change and the ability to make the change are critical to the flow of the match and to the final outcome.

BATTLE #2: FORCING AN OPPONENT INTO A NEGATIVE FRAME OF MIND

The second battle relates to the emotional state of mind of each player. *The player's goal is to gain control of the match by changing his opponent's positive attitude into a negative one as quickly as possible.*

A player needs to win key points and games, and either get ahead or stay close in the score to maintain a high level of confidence. An opponent who struggles to stay close will become more and more concerned about how he is going to win, and will probably begin to make unforced errors because he will start going for too much on his shots.

Next, mental errors will creep in. At this point, his opponent is losing confidence and is beginning to move into a lower intensity level. He is starting to doubt his ability to compete in the match. He still has the potential to win, but he cannot allow himself to lose any more self-confidence.

The smart player never reaches this low level because he keeps fighting for every point as he looks for answers and adjustments to turn things around. This mentally astute player realizes that it is also the goal of his opponent to have the player enter a negative frame of mind. He knows he has to guard against becoming negative, and must stay positive even if his shots do not fall in.

OVERCOMING PRESSURE

One crucial bit of advice: *when feeling pressure, the player should remind himself to try to relax, so his muscles can flow naturally and smoothly through the swing.* One way to do this: find a reason to smile or laugh. Many top professional players do this when they feel nervous to help them break the tension.

TURNING THE OPPONENT'S FRUSTRATION INTO ANGER

If the opponent is struggling with his game and is experiencing discouragement and a loss of confidence, the player wants to maintain the pressure he is exerting with each point. He wants to see his opponent's discouragement turn to frustration or anger. The player can accomplish this by:

- ▸▸ Exposing and playing shots toward his opponent's weakness
- ▸▸ Negating his strength
- ▸▸ Beating him consistently with winning shots and winners
- ▸▸ Forcing his opponent to play a level higher than he is capable of playing that day.

The opponent's frustration will deepen as he realizes he is beating himself due to mental errors, unforced errors, and missed opportunities. Increasing inner tension affects the natural movement of his muscles, which need to be relaxed in order to execute well-timed shots. Tension from pressure, frustration, and anger throws off his timing. Also, he is spending valuable time on negative thoughts instead of coaching himself back into the next point.

If a player keeps his intensity level high while maintaining constant pressure on his demoralized opponent, he will attain the goal of winning this battle and will likely win the match. Few players can blow off their anger and come back to play a great point. An opponent's anger will start feeding on itself as he loses both confidence and concentration. He is giving up control of his head and can be dominated in this lower intensity level.

It is important to note that when an opponent gets into this state, *a player need not hit winners.* A player can ensure his victory with consistent strokes, as his opponent has such low intensity, concentration, and confidence that he is increasingly vulnerable.

BATTLE #3: PUSHING AN OPPONENT BEYOND HIS PHYSICAL TOLERANCE

The third battle involves physical endurance. Each player begins the match with an energy level based on his conditioning, his health, and the amount of previous play. Each player also has a physical tolerance level at which fatigue begins to affect him. *The goal of this third battle is to push his opponent to that level as quickly as possible, because fatigue will alter his timing, concentration, and ability to compete in a match.*

Some ways to wear down an opponent include:
- Playing longer rallies
- Hitting away from an opponent, forcing him to run as much as possible for difficult angles
- Stretching him high and low for shots
- Making him hit overheads, which take the most energy of any shot.

It is just as important to push an opponent to exert himself physically as it is to win each point. Figure 1 describes the importance of the different distances the player wants to make his opponent move:
- Quarter Court (6–7 feet): the minimum distance; places the opponent in an off-centered position; good for conservative shots like service returns and first shots in a baseline rally.
- Half Court (13–14 feet): the average distance; moves the opponent from a centered baseline position into a vulnerable position in the corner.
- Three-Quarter Court (20–21 feet): a more tiring distance; player uses this distance to take and maintain control of the point.
- Full Court (beyond 21 feet): the optimal distance to tire out the opponent the quickest; even a quick player has trouble running corner to corner, running down short balls and drop shots inside the service boxes, and retrieving lobs.

FIGURE 1
Moving Your Opponent

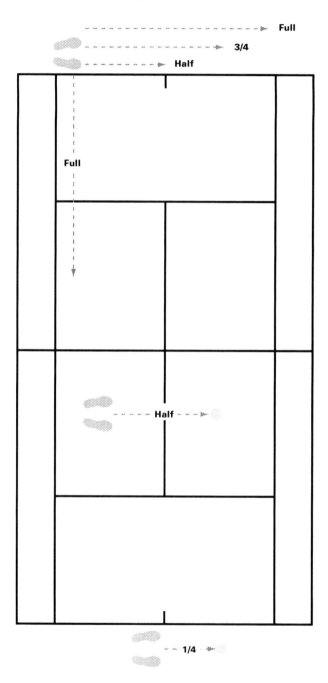

SPOTTING FATIGUE

It helps to know how to spot fatigue. A few signs of fatigue in an opponent are not hard to detect:

- ▶ He starts missing easy shots
- ▶ The pace on his shots slows down
- ▶ He fails to reach balls he was getting to earlier in the match
- ▶ His first-serve percentage slips
- ▶ He starts taking more time to get ready between points and games.

The player's goal is to have his opponent feeling fatigued toward the end of the second set. The trick is to get him to this point before the player reaches it himself.

GUARD AGAINST SELF-DOUBT

The player's potential to attack his opponent on all three fronts depends upon his ability to control his own head. He must guard continuously against negative forces such as frustration, anger, and negative self-talk. *No one can play successfully against two people—his opponent and himself—and still expect to win.*

The player who has a positive mental approach to the game believes in his ability to compete. He has confidence in his strokes and knows that he can find a way to win because he has done it in the past and can do it again. He realizes that if he shows frustration or anger, it will boost the confidence of his opponent. The smart player always projects the image that he is in control (through his body language) and can win the match even if he is not playing his best tennis. This player is aware that a philosophy based on positive thinking will help him achieve his goals on the court.

The challenge of a smart player is to attack his opponent on all three fronts. He is always aware of his opponent's vulnerabilities and knows to take advantage of them to wear him down emotionally, physically and strategically. *It is usually easiest to attack his opponent emotionally.* Once emotions take over, he continues to work on his physical capability, and having won that battle, the player has all but won the match. He practices using this "battle" plan and becomes more proficient at recognizing when he is winning any of the battles. With each success he gains more and more confidence to take into future matches.

4

Secrets to Mental Toughness

INTENSITY COMES IN TWO FORMS: MENTAL AND PHYSICAL AND BOTH ARE equally important to maintain in a match. The player who can maintain a high level of intensity throughout a match will have success playing aggressively, and will be hard to beat. His stroke consistency, placement, pace, and shot variety will be affected by his intensity level, as well as his ability to compete, to self-coach, and to develop a strategy for winning points.

SECRET #1 · LEARNING TO CONCENTRATE

Mental intensity is dependent upon concentration and confidence. Concentration is the ability to focus all mental energy in a positive manner toward winning points and is one of the most difficult things to develop in tennis. At the highest levels of concentration, the player avoids mental errors, plays more creative and aggressive points, and commits few unforced errors. The smart player is aware that every point has significance to the outcome of the match, and so, regardless of the score, he will compete for every point.

KEYS TO CONCENTRATION

The key to concentrating effectively is learning how to self-coach. It is likely that the player's mind will wander if not stimulated by a constant self-coaching dialogue before, during, and after points—and also between games.

There are two critical questions the player must ask himself in order to self-coach effectively: *What am I doing well?* and *What do I need to do better to win the match?*

READING THE BALL

To compete at a high level, players need to have a purpose for every shot they hit and they must learn to read the ball as it comes off their opponent's racquet. Reading the ball is a tricky exercise that takes a lot of skill, concentration, and practice. It involves analyzing the ball's movement, spin, and varying depths. Good ball reading requires the player to *focus continuously on the ball* as it comes off his opponent's racquet and continue to track it as it leaves his racquet.

As his opponent strokes the ball, the player should determine the *direction* and the *pace* of the ball, plus the *height* by which the ball will clear the net. These variables will reveal where the ball will bounce, how high it will bounce and how much time the player will have to reach it. The spin on the ball will indicate what kind of bounce to expect. If he is able to analyze these variables by the time the ball travels over his opponent's service line, he will have enough time to reach most shots.

The player must determine if the ball is rising or descending when it crosses the net. If the ball is rising, it will carry to the backcourt. If it is descending, in most cases it will bounce in the service box and take a quick second bounce. If the ball is not read properly, he will not reach it in time to make a good play. His ability to move his feet and get into a favorable position to hit the ball will depend on how well he learns to concentrate and read the ball. *A good reading combined with good anticipation can make up for a lack of quickness in foot speed.*

READING HIS SHOT

To maintain his concentration, the player must also read the flight of the ball as it leaves his racquet. This will reveal how well or how poorly he hit that particular shot. He needs to detect what error he made so he can make the appropriate adjustment on his next shot.

LISTENING TO THE BALL

There will be times when the eyes alone are not enough to impart information, and the player will need to rely on his ears to help. There are several particular situations in which the ears can transfer information more quickly than the eyes:

- ▸ The ears can pick up the sound of a mis-hit before a player realizes the shot was hit poorly;
- ▸ The ears can help determine the pace of a shot by the sound of the

ball contacting his opponent's racquet. The harder hit ball produces a louder sound;

▸▸ The ears can help differentiate between a flat or spin serve because each produces a different sound as it comes off the server's racquet. A flat serve produces a sharp cracking sound, while a spin serve produces a more muffled sound where you can actually hear the racquet brush the ball.

HAVING A PURPOSE FOR EACH SHOT

Every player should have a purpose for each shot he hits. This purpose may be offensive, defensive, or neutral. Between points, a player should mentally rehearse the previous point and consider any adjustments he needs to make. He must prepare mentally for the upcoming point by analyzing the importance of the next point for himself and for his opponent, and develop a plan for each point beforehand.

Between games, the player should analyze his tactics, his intensity level, and the tactics of his opponent. If he is thinking constantly, his mind will stay sharp, stimulated, and focused.

SECRET #2 • DEVELOPING CONFIDENCE

Gaining confidence both within a match and from match to match is critical. Showing improvement and reaching goals helps to create confidence, but winning matches is the foundation upon which confidence is built. The player's matches will provide him with the knowledge of what needs to be improved or added to his game to make him an even more successful competitor.

STAYING POSITIVE

The mentally tough player understands that by staying positive he will keep his intensity at a higher level, which will enable him to make more of his shots until he has his chance to go ahead. He knows that negative thoughts will destroy his confidence and block his ability to concentrate. This attitude will help him succeed in turning matches around for victories. Once he accomplishes a come-from-behind win, his confidence will increase and it will be easier to come back in future matches.

FIVE EFFECTS OF CONFIDENCE

Confidence and positive thinking are the keys to the mentally tough player's ability. Confidence will allow the player to:

- ⏩ Raise the level of his game
- ⏩ Take risks on crucial points and in crucial stages of a match
- ⏩ Relax during stressful situations
- ⏩ Develop momentum
- ⏩ Provide the edge in a match.

SECRET #3 · CREATING PHYSICAL INTENSITY

Physical intensity, which derives from the player's physical movements, is another component of his intensity level. The player can have perfect stroke technique, but he will not win points if he cannot get to the ball. The more quickly he gets to the ball, the more preparation time he will have. With more time to prepare, he will find it easier to time his shots. Good physical movement includes quickness, body agility, hustle, stamina, and good footwork. The player's level of physical intensity will be determined by the strength of these five elements of movement.

1 QUICKNESS

It is difficult to make a genetically slow person fast, but his quickness can be improved with the proper instruction and training. It is important to incorporate speed work into drills and conditioning exercises. Players must combine quickness with good footwork so they do not overrun balls and create errors. Quickness adds confidence and will be a great asset to a player's game. His opponent will fear the player's speed and will feel as if he has to hit a better shot all the time to win each point. This will result in more unforced errors by his opponent. *The player can appear to be quick if he combines average speed with good footwork and a good reading of the ball.*

2 BODY AGILITY

Body agility is the skillful control of body movements. A good sense of balance and the ability to change direction quickly are both essential for the player who might find his legs moving in one direction while his upper body needs to move in the opposite direction. The need for agility becomes most apparent at the net, where quick responses are necessary continuously. The player can improve his body agility with proper conditioning exercises.

3 HUSTLE

Hustle is the player's use of maximum physical effort. *He competes physically through an optimal use of hustle, especially on the big points.* The player who hustles has his muscles working at peak capacity. He is further energized by the thought that he was able to reach a particularly difficult shot, and his physical intensity increases even further. All players have the ability to hustle, but they have to be in excellent shape to continue at a high level throughout a match. The smart player knows that hustle can make the difference in four to six points in a match, and these points should help win at least one game. Points won through hustle might occur in a crucial game and might provide the difference in a very close match.

An interesting aspect of hustle is that a player doesn't have to win a point to have his hustle pay off. Getting close to the ball provides two messages. First, the player knows he can reach that ball the next time. Second, his opponent realizes that he almost reached the ball and therefore, that shot might not be enough to win the next time. This thinking might cause him to go for more than is necessary, and might result in an unforced error. Hustle can turn around games, sets, and matches. It helps to keep the player in a high intensity level, and it also can bring the player up from low intensity.

4 STAMINA

Stamina provides the player with the capability to compete at a high level of physical intensity throughout the match. It is developed through hard play and a strenuous conditioning program of the many different muscle groups in the body that are essential in competitive tennis. One of the most overlooked muscle groups is the eye muscles. They must be developed and conditioned so they will be able to continue focusing on the ball during a long rally and a long match. Patience alone is not sufficient to win long baseline rallies. The eye muscles must be able to concentrate on the ball continuously. Strong eye muscles can be developed through reading the ball and playing long rallies in practice.

5 GOOD FOOTWORK

Good footwork is essential. *Movement stimulates the brain and keeps the player more aggressive physically and mentally.* When movement precedes ball contact, the timing of the shot improves. It is important for players to keep their feet moving in preparation for every shot they are about to receive. And the "split-step" is a very important aspect of proper footwork. Players must bounce lightly on the balls of their feet every time an opponent strikes the ball. This movement helps prepare a player for whatever shot his opponent might hit next.

SECRET #4 • WARMING UP PROPERLY

It is important for the player to break a sweat and to get his muscles warmed up as quickly as possible in a match. The longer the rallies at the start of the match, the more quickly his muscles will warm up and the more quickly he will feel in the flow of the point. Short points are detrimental to getting in the flow. When short points are occurring, he must remind himself to get his feet moving before the next point starts. This can be accomplished by running in place for five or six steps or by bouncing up and down on both feet. Any body movement prior to the start of the point will prepare the brain and raise his intensity level before the point begins. Movement will also send a message to his opponent that he is ready to play the point.

A player's intensity level influences nearly every aspect of competitive play. A player must learn how to maintain a high level of mental and physical intensity throughout each match. He must constantly monitor them and make adjustments so that he is always competing at his highest level.

Any player who gets into the habit of using his inner coach between points and games, practices reading the ball to build concentration skills, and hustles for every ball will improve his chances of winning matches.

5

Playing Percentage Tennis

MOST POINTS IN A MATCH ARE WON ON ERRORS, NOT WINNERS. REGARDLESS of a player's ability level, he can increase his chances for success if he reduces his number of unforced errors by keeping a high percentage of shots in play. To do this effectively, he must understand percentage tennis and how it influences his shot selection.

CONTROLLED AGGRESSIVENESS

Percentage tennis is choosing to hit the most effective shot for the situation. Before each shot the player must consider how aggressive he can be without sacrificing control because every shot carries a risk-versus-reward decision. If there is too great a risk in hitting an aggressive shot, the smart player will settle for a lesser shot to keep the ball in play. He must combine his first priority of keeping the ball in play (control), with his second objective of setting up or winning the point with his shot (aggressiveness). If he is able to reach the delicate balance between these two objectives, he then will be playing percentage tennis with *controlled aggressiveness*.

Playing with controlled aggressiveness is challenging because there are many things for the player to consider in the relatively short time between shots. Some of the main factors that will affect shot selection are:

- ▸▸ The player's and his opponent's intensity levels
- ▸▸ The pace, angle, depth, and spin of the oncoming ball
- ▸▸ The player's position and his opponent's position on the court
- ▸▸ The score of the game and the score in the match.

Keeping the ball in play sounds like an easy task. It isn't. For that reason, it is essential that the player understand the interaction of four variables that determine whether or not the ball stays in play: pace, direction, height (clearance over the net), and spin.

There are limits as to how much of each variable the player can mix together and still keep his shot in play. For example:

1 A ball hit too softly and too low will go into the net

2 A ball hit with too much angle and pace will go wide

3 A ball hit too high over the net might be difficult to keep inside the baseline, depending on the pace and spin of the ball

4 A ball hit with too much pace might go long unless sufficient topspin is added to the shot. Topspin increases the player's ability to control the ball. The harder the player wants to hit the ball, the more topspin he needs to use to keep the ball in play.

MARGINS FOR ERROR

Understanding and using margins for error, or safety margins, will build insurance into each shot, and will help the player keep his shot under control while he increases the chance of winning the point. There are three basic margins that need to be considered:

1 The distance of the ball above the headband as it goes over the net

2 The distance inside the baseline the ball lands

3 The distance from the sideline the ball lands

The player must decide at what distance above the net headband he wants to hit his shot. The higher the player aims his shot over the net, the less likely the ball will hit the net, and the more conservative the shot is. The lower the ball is aimed over the net, the more aggressive the shot is, and the greater the risk factor.

The second margin for error is the distance the ball lands inside the baseline. The third margin is the distance the ball lands from the singles sideline. *The closer to the baseline and the sideline the ball lands, the more aggressive and effective a shot is (and the more likely his opponent will make an error).* However, a greater risk is involved in the more aggressive shot. The farther the ball lands from these two lines, the more conservative is the shot.

DECIDING THE BEST SHOT TO HIT

Many errors are caused by improper shot selection. There are times within a point to stay under control and there are times to be aggressive. Smart players know which ball dictates which situation, and this helps them win more points. Generally, when his opponent hits an aggressive shot (very deep, hard, or both), the player should respond with a neutral shot, or a defensive shot to try to stay in the point. If his opponent hits a weaker shot (short, slow, or both), the player should answer with an aggressive shot (such as hard and deep or hard and angled).

A common error in match play is the attempt to hit a great shot instead of going with a good, high percentage shot that could also be successful. The difference between the two shots is the margin for error built into each, and the potential for losing the point with the great shot, and winning the point with the higher percentage shot.

CONSERVATIVE VS. AGGRESSIVE: A FEW EXAMPLES

There is always a range of conservative to aggressive shots that can be used effectively in a given situation. A conservative clearance margin for the advanced player, when both he and his opponent are on the baseline, would be a minimum of two feet to avoid hitting a ball into the net. Any shot under two feet in this situation would have an aggressive clearance margin. *A smart player would consider it a mental error to hit a ball into the net during a baseline rally.*

If his opponent is at the net, the player should hit his passing shot between one and two feet over the net for a conservative margin, and under one foot clearance for an aggressive shot. An effective, aggressive approach shot also should stay under one foot of clearance to have the best chance of staying in the court.

SHOT ZONES

The aggressive shot zone for the advanced player includes the area four feet inside the baseline, and three feet inside the singles sidelines. Any ball that lands in this aggressive shot zone has a small margin for error; because of the greater risk involved, more errors will occur on shots hit to this zone. These shots will also force more errors on many opponents.

The conservative shot zone is from four to nine feet inside the baseline, and from three to seven feet from each singles sideline. Any shot that lands in this area is a safer shot because there is a greater margin for error. The downside is that shots hit to this zone will not force many errors unless hit hard.

PLAY IT SAFE

The beauty of hitting a shot to the conservative zone is that the player has built in insurance against over hitting the ball. Consider Figure 2. A player wants to hit the ball to location A, which is six feet from the baseline and six feet from the singles sideline. If he is hitting the ball down the line and slightly over hits it, the ball will land at **B**. If he is hitting this ball crosscourt and slightly over hits it, the ball will land at **C**. Both of these were over-hit shots, but each landed in the court, and actually became better shots than what the player had intended to hit. Thanks to the insurance factor built into the conservative shot, he unexpectedly hit a more aggressive shot. *This concept becomes especially significant when playing the big points.*

Less experienced players should hit all their shots with extra clearance over the net, and to his opponent's backcourt (the area between the service line and the baseline). They should use over four feet of net clearance for conservative margins and less than four feet for aggressive shots. Their aggressive shot zone is the back half of the backcourt (within nine feet of the baseline), and within seven feet of the singles sidelines. Everything else is conservative.

In Figure 3, three possible shots, **A**, **B** and **C**, can be evaluated in terms of percentage tennis. All three are hit by the player to the same side of the court, and all force his opponent to hit an angled ball from an off-centered position. Yet, each carries a different risk.

Shot **A** is the most conservative of the three because it has the greatest margin for error and therefore, the best chance of staying in play. It may cause an unforced error, but would need to be hit with good pace to force an error. Shot **A** is the least likely of these three shots to win points. It has the least amount of angle on the ball, and his opponent will have to run the shortest distance to return this shot. He should be able to reach this ball in time to plant his feet and hit a good balanced shot. Unless it were kept low, shot **A** would not be a good shot to hit to his opponent's strength. However, it would be a good first groundstroke after serving, or a good target for a service return.

Shot **B** has a nice blend of risk and reward. It is more aggressive than A, and is more likely to force an error, especially if it is hit with good pace. Although it has less margin for error than **A**, it is a much higher percentage shot when compared to **C**. The angle the ball takes for Shot **B** is greater than that of **A**, and

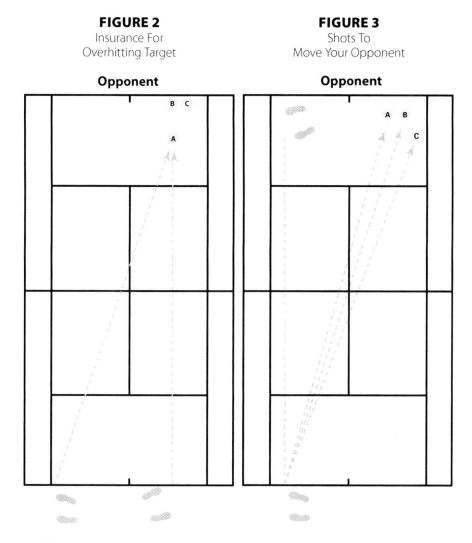

FIGURE 2
Insurance For
Overhitting Target

FIGURE 3
Shots To
Move Your Opponent

will force his opponent to run a further distance. He will probably get to this ball also, but he may have to hit it on the run, and possibly at the last second, which could result in a lesser shot. Unlike Shot **A**, Shot **B** will be effective even when hitting to his opponent's strength. It is a good choice to use on big points, and also when the player is determined to dictate the point.

Shot **C** has the widest angle of these shots, and will make his opponent run the furthest distance to reach the ball. Although it provides the greatest chance to win the point through a forced error or a winner, Shot **C** also carries the greatest risk. It is an aggressive shot with virtually no margin for error. It must be attempted *only* when the player is in high intensity. The player has to hit **C** at a slower pace than **A** or **B** to increase its probability of staying in play. Shot **C** would be a good choice against a quick player because it expands the court well. A less risky shot, such as **B**, would pressure the opponent's timing and be a sufficient alternative, especially when playing big points.

WHEN TO PLAY CONSERVATIVELY

- ▸ During the first game of a match. It is important for the player to keep the ball in play in this game and force his opponent to beat him in order to win each point. The player wants to use the first game to assess his opponent and also to start getting a good feel for the ball.
- ▸ On the first groundstroke or first volley after hitting a serve. The player needs to use this shot to get the feel of the ball and also to get into the flow of the point. The longer the time delay between points, the more important this becomes.
- ▸ When the player wants to change the angle of the incoming ball by a substantial degree. *The more the angle is changed, the greater the risk of making an error.*
- ▸ When the player hits a particular shot for the first time in a match, such as a first volley, overhead, or approach shot.
- ▸ When the difference between the pace of the incoming ball and the outgoing shot varies greatly.
- ▸ When the player wants to change the spin of the incoming ball.
- ▸ When the player has to hit the ball on the dead run and he needs to compensate for his body momentum.
- ▸ When the player is in low intensity. He will create more errors for himself if he tries to be too aggressive.

WHEN TO PLAY AGGRESSIVELY

1 When the player needs to expand the court against a quick opponent or one with a good reach.
2 When his opponent is a better player. The player will have to take more risks to play at a higher level because his conservative shots are not enough to beat this opponent.
3 When the player is having trouble breaking serve. A player may need to take more risk either on the early points and/or on the break points to get his service break.

4 When the player wants to keep his opponent on the baseline and make it difficult for him to come to the net.

OVERCOMING FATIGUE AND PRESSURE

The two factors that greatly decrease the player's percentages in a match are fatigue and pressure. Both directly affect the player's timing, and both often come into play together at critical times in a match. Good self-coaching techniques can help to overcome the negative impact of fatigue and pressure.

Many players commit errors because of tired shots and do not realize it immediately. A smart player anticipates symptoms of fatigue, recognizes them, and begins to make the proper adjustments. He knows that fatigue will cause him to be a half step late to the shot, which will make it difficult to set his feet, and will force him to hit on the run. This, in turn, will add more pressure to the execution of the shot. To correct this problem, the player should self-coach by reminding himself to try to get a quicker read on the ball and hustle more so that he might be able to set his feet for his shot. If the player is too tired to do this, he must add extra sideline and baseline margin to compensate for hitting the ball on the run. Or, he may also want to get to the net where he can play shorter points.

Fatigue also causes balls to land shorter in the court. This allows an opponent to play more aggressively. When this starts to happen, a player should remind himself to accelerate his swing and/or add to the clearance margin so the ball will carry deeper into the backcourt.

Pressure will shrink margins, sometimes as much as 50%. Under stress, a player should increase the topspin he puts on the ball to control his shots. He should also add other precautions to his game. For example, a player often might want to hit a passing shot one foot over the net and three feet inside the sideline. To compensate for pressure, he should hit the ball closer to two feet over the net and aim about five feet from the sideline.

Playing the percentages will result in more wins for any player. The smart player learns to use controlled aggressiveness in his matches as he realizes what he must do to balance the reward of hitting winning shots with the risk of missing. In playing percentage tennis, he will always be thinking of the most effective shot for the situation, and his chances for success increase automatically.

6

Point Development

Tennis is like a game of chess. The player can wait patiently until his opponent makes a mistake and then capitalize on it, or he can take a more aggressive approach and plan out a progression of moves that will win the point. These choices illustrate the concept of point development, which is the key to making good strokes more productive. Point development is the process of combining shots in a sequence to win points through unforced errors, forced errors, and winners. The sequence of shots can occur within one point or in different points when linked together to create a pattern.

The goal of point development is to win each point and simultaneously work toward winning each of the three battles (developing a winning strategy, forcing an opponent into a negative state of mind, and pushing him beyond his physical tolerance—as discussed in Chapter 3). A player can accomplish this by challenging his opponent's concentration, by hitting difficult shots that create pressure on his timing, by exhausting his energy, and by using winning tactics.

The player must have a plan for each point before it is played or he will set himself up for failure. If he is the server he must decide if he is going to serve and volley, serve and rally from the baseline, or serve and come in on the first opportunity. If he is returning serve he must decide if he is going to come to the net off his return, rally from the baseline, or come in on short or weak shots. If he chooses to stay on the baseline, the player must decide if he wants to bring his opponent in to the net or try to keep him on the baseline. His decisions should be based on the score at the time, his and his opponent's intensity level, and what has happened in the previous points in the game.

THE SEVEN WEAPONS

There are seven point development weapons a player can use to gain an advantage over his opponent. As a player combines these weapons he puts additional pressure on his opponent's timing and increases his chances of winning the point with a forced error or a winner. Smart players understand the value and the role these weapons play in good point development.

WEAPON #1 • SPIN

The smart player can alternate spins or set up different patterns of spins on his groundstrokes. Topspin and underspin are the two most widely used spins and are very effective because the height of the bounce can be varied on both. Topspin kicks high on an opponent and accelerates after the bounce, which makes shots difficult to time. A shoulder-high ball doesn't give an opponent much to work with. A weak return often follows.

There are various types of bounces underspin can produce. A shot can have so much backspin on it that the ball will bounce straight up at impact. A drop shot will actually change directions after bouncing. Another type of underspin can flatten out at impact, stay below his opponent's hitting zone, and skid toward a quick second bounce. This pushes an opponent to move more quickly and diminishes his reaction time. It also forces his opponent to hit a shot at or below knee level where the net becomes more of an obstacle. This is particularly effective when playing against an opponent who uses a low net clearance. It can also be a smart choice against a tall opponent because he has to bend down so far to reach his shots.

WEAPON #2 • PACE

The smart player will vary the pace of his shots from slow to fast. Changing the pace will challenge his opponent's timing because he will have to constantly shift his preparation time for each shot. His opponent will have more time to prepare for a ball hit at a slower pace, and less time to prepare for a faster ball. Slow shots must be deep enough or low enough so that an opponent can't easily put them away.

Adding pace to well-placed shots forces an opponent to hit defensive shots. Additional pace on the ball also forces errors and creates winners. If controlled, it is a significant weapon and can intimidate an opponent. However, *pace must be used with caution and good margins.* Using good margins allows the smart player to hit the ball harder with confidence because he knows his shot has a better chance of staying in play.

WEAPON #3 • DEPTH

The closer the ball lands to the baseline, the more difficult it is to return. Balls hit within two feet of the baseline are effective because his opponent either has to take the ball on the rise, which demands better timing, or retreat deeper behind the baseline, which puts him at a disadvantage to retrieve shorter or angled shots. As a general rule, the smart player should keep the ball as deep as possible so he will have more time to read and react to his opponent's shot. This is also more likely to force his opponent into hitting a shorter ball, giving the player an opportunity to be more aggressive.

Changing the depth of each shot affects his opponent's timing. He will have more time to prepare for the shorter shots and less time for the deeper shots. This change in preparation time can lead to unforced errors. The player needs to be cautious on the short ball especially if his opponent handles it well. He may only want to hit the short ball when he wants to bring his opponent in to the net on his terms and is mentally prepared to hit a passing shot or a lob. A good short ball is an underspin shot that descends as it crosses over the net because the ball will stay low and take a quick second bounce.

WEAPON #4 • ANGLE

A ball traveling straight ahead toward a player is often the easiest shot to play. A player should try to hit most balls on some kind of angle, forcing his opponent to concentrate harder and increasing the possibility of an unforced error. He now has to read each angle, decide the appropriate place to plant his feet for the shot, and what contact point he wants to use. These decisions will become even more difficult under pressure or when he is feeling fatigued.

Angled shots move either toward his opponent or away from him. Both types of angles are effective, but the best angles move away from an opponent. They expand the court, making his opponent run farther and placing him farther away from a centered position. Shots that are continuously angled away from his opponent will force him to expend an enormous amount of energy as he has farther and farther to run in order to retrieve the next shot. An angled shot is most effective when combined with another angled shot in the opposite direction. *The hardest shot for an opponent to handle is one hit on the run below knee level and angled to his weaker side.* Not only is it difficult to time, but it also forces him to hit a defensive shot.

WEAPON #5 • PROXIMITY

The closer the player can get to his opponent when hitting a shot, the greater his advantage. His opponent will feel more pressure and have less time to prepare because the player's shot will come back more quickly. Also, as the player closes in, his opponent is forced to move to the ball more rapidly.

Figure 4 shows three general areas of the court from which the player can strike the ball. Proximity provides the greatest advantage from **A** because he has the choice of a wider variety of angles to hit his shot. Proximity is also a factor in these match situations:

▸▸ When his opponent is playing from the baseline and the player is able to move in to the area between **B** and **C** to hit the shot;

▸▸ When his opponent is at the net and the player is able to hit his passing shot or lob from the area between the baseline and **C**.

The most widely used application of this weapon from the baseline is the technique of taking the ball on the rise, or immediately after it bounces. The player uses this shot either because he does not have time to retreat behind the baseline, or because he chooses to play aggressively from the baseline. The smart player is always looking for an opportunity to move forward to gain an advantage through Proximity.

WEAPON #6 • EXPLOITING VULNERABLE POSITIONS

A player can string together smart combinations of shots from the baseline, which challenge his opponent's hands, footwork, speed, and stamina. He can accomplish this by putting an opponent in a vulnerable position in the following situations:

▸▸ When an opponent is positioned behind the baseline, he is often vulnerable to a good drop shot;

▸▸ When an opponent is in either corner he will be vulnerable to a ball hit to the opposite corner;

▸▸ When an opponent is in a good volley position at the net, he will be vulnerable to a lob.

By executing the proper shot in the above situations, the player can exploit his opponent's vulnerable position. *A winning combination often comes when a player can get close to the net and take advantage of his opponent being out of position.*

WEAPON #7 • SURPRISE

The smart player is creative in his point development. He uses his creativity to "surprise" his opponent with a shot that is different from what would be expected

FIGURE 4
Court Positions

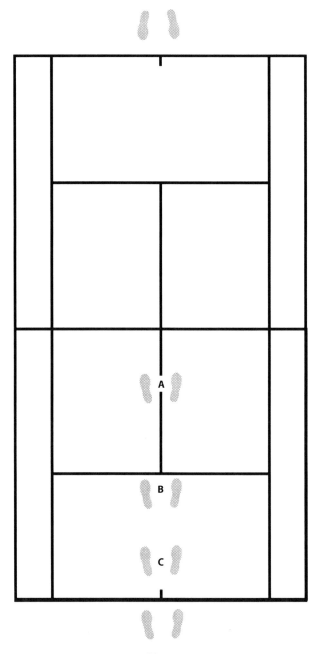

Player

in the given situation. Winning points by surprise, the smart player frustrates and intimidates his opponent. He becomes more and more uncomfortable and worries about what will happen next. He begins to doubt himself and to believe the player is more clever than he is on the court.

CONSTRUCTING THE POINT

The first opportunity the player has to win a point is with the serve or the service return. He may win the point outright with either shot, which is the optimal method, for he exerts the least amount of energy in doing so. If he does not win the point with the serve or the return, he must use groundstrokes to develop the point.

BASIC COMPONENTS

Two basic components all players must have firmly in their game are *steadiness and alternating sides*. Every point will contain these two essentials of point development. *Steadiness is the basic component of all point play and the prerequisite for successful point development.* The smart player understands he cannot work, dictate, or finish the point if he can't keep the ball in play. Steadiness depends on the following factors:

- Hustle
- Making stroke adjustments though good self-coaching techniques
- Choosing good targets through an understanding of margins
- Selecting appropriate shots (offensive, neutral, or defensive) for the situation using percentage tennis
- Keeping unforced errors to a minimum by concentrating.

This last point might sound obvious, but it is crucial. Many opponents have a mental limit as to how long they can stay focused on each individual point. They might dislike the type of shot they have to play, fail to focus on the stroke adjustment necessary on a particular shot, or even lose interest in playing long points. A smart player capitalizes on all these things.

He will want to alternate the groundstrokes he makes an opponent hit. The goal is to make an opponent alternate from forehand to backhand as much as possible so he is always hitting a different stroke. This requires different footwork, contact points, and grips. The player can also use various patterns of forehands and backhands to further challenge his concentration. For example, he might hit two backhands and then one forehand or three forehands followed by two backhands. He strives to take an opponent out of his comfort zone.

All too often, less experienced players especially, attempt to use pace before they have full command of consistency and placement. Only after a player is consistent with his shots and has the ability to place the ball to different areas of the court, is he able to use the seven weapons effectively. Only then is he ready to consider the approaches to constructing a point.

There are two approaches to baseline groundstroke point development: *working the point and dictating the point*. A player can use either approach to win the point, or he can combine the approaches by first working the point and then shift into dictating the point. In each approach, the player is looking for an opportunity which will allow him ultimately to win the point. The player must master both approaches to constructing a point if he hopes to attain a high level of play.

WORK THE POINT

The more conservative approach is for the player to be patient and work the point. He must expect the point will take longer to win. He will use the weapons of spin, pace, depth, and angle as he works to outsteady his opponent. The focus of this approach is to challenge his opponent's timing by varying the spins, the pace, the depths, and the angles of each shot. The smart player combines these weapons to create additional pressure on his opponent's shots. Examples of good combinations would be heavy topspin with good depth, underspin with good angle, and topspin with good pace. Combining three and four weapons together increases the likelihood of a forced error or winner. Combining these weapons with steadiness and alternating sides, he is now challenging his opponent's timing as well as his concentration. He can combine different weapons so his opponent never sees the same shot twice in a row. His opponent will be kept off-balance and will have a difficult time getting his groundstrokes grooved. A player will use this approach to point development:

▸▸ When he is in low intensity (and wants to raise it)

▸▸ During the first point of a game to get into the flow

▸▸ During the first few games of the match (when he is trying to feel out his opponent)

▸▸ When he is behind in the game score

▸▸ To begin critical points.

The goal of working the point is to get an unforced error or one of the following **opportunities***:*

▸▸ He should look for a ball that he can hit with his best shot. Ideally, he strives to hit his best shot as often as possible in a match;

▸▸ He should look for a ball that is moving toward him at a slower pace than the previous shot or two. This slower ball allows for additional preparation time, which makes it easier to execute a shot with more pace, better angle, more depth, or to change spins;

▸▸ He should look for a ball that lands shorter in the court than the previous shot or two. This shorter ball allows the player to be more aggressive and offensive in his shot because he will have additional preparation time. The player will have proximity working for him.

Note: The player might also use any of these opportunities to take control from an opponent who has been dictating or controlling the point. If the player has been on the defensive, he will want to look for an opportunity to start dictating play. He must anticipate well and be ready to take advantage of any opportunity that occurs.

It is important for the player to anticipate the situations that might lead to an opportunity, such as:

▸▸ Hitting a shot to his opponent's weaker groundstroke or to the side he is struggling with in the match

▸▸ Using the weapon that is creating the most errors

▸▸ Looking for a ball mis-hit by his opponent

▸▸ Noticing when his opponent is late striking the ball

▸▸ Looking for a ball that is struck below the knees or above his opponent's shoulder.

As soon as any of these situations occur, the player should realize he might have an opportunity and he must be ready to take advantage of it.

DICTATE THE POINT

The more aggressive approach of point development is to *dictate the point*. If a player intends to be the aggressor in his baseline point development, his main objective is to take control of each point. A player wins most of his points because he has good command of his shots, which enables him to dictate the flow of the point. He is constantly looking for opportunities to be more aggressive and to take control of the point. He will expend less energy than his opponent as he controls the movement of the ball and attempts to run him continuously corner to corner on the court. If successful, he will take away his opponent's ability to be as aggressive and offensive as he might wish.

The player will have the *best* opportunity to take control of the point once he has his opponent off a centered position and in a baseline corner.

Therefore, the player should hit to either his opponent's forehand or backhand corner as quickly as possible to create a position of vulnerability. He has the best opportunity to accomplish this when his opponent hits his shot down the center of the court from a centered position. This is the optimal position from which the player can hit a shot, for there is always a good option from there.

The player has the potential to start taking control of the point by hitting away from his opponent in either direction with many angles from which to choose. He should consider hitting to the corner of his opponent's weaker side. The player's shot to either corner from a centered position requires a minimal change in the angle which will make the timing of the shot less demanding. Also, the player remains in a centered position for his opponent's next shot, which means he will have to move at most only half-court for it. Finally, he is able to conserve energy while his opponent has to exert more energy. This is the only position on the court where all these factors work in his favor.

If both the player and his opponent are not in centered positions on the baseline, the player must consider hitting to his open corner. This will force him to run the furthest distance for the shot. His body position will determine to which corner the ball should be hit. If he is to the left of center, the appropriate shot would be to the right corner because he would have to run the farthest distance to reach the ball. (Of course, if he is to the right of center, the next shot should be to his left corner). The player must be careful about the pace with which he hits if he is in the corner. If he hits with too much pace, he will reduce the amount of time he will have to re-center himself or run to his opposite corner, and so his opponent could use the additional pace on his ball against him. The player should choose to hit a slower ball which will enable him to recover to a centered position.

Once the player has his opponent in a vulnerable position in a corner, he can now take control of the point. He will hit to the opposite corner to keep him vulnerable and make him run the farthest distance for each shot. He will maintain control of the point by continuously running him corner to corner (full court). He is forced to run faster and farther on the court for each shot which adds to the difficulty in timing the ball he must hit and he expends a significant amount of energy in the process. The player also could choose to mix-up the spins, pace, depths, and angles of his shots to further challenge his timing. He may use any or all of the seven weapons in dictating the point.

A player will use this approach to point development:

- ▸▸ When he is in high intensity
- ▸▸ To keep pressure on his opponent
- ▸▸ When he has momentum
- ▸▸ When he is ahead in the game score
- ▸▸ After his good serve forces a weak return
- ▸▸ After he hits a well-placed return to a baseline corner.

The goals of dictating the point are:

- ▸▸ To put his opponent on the defensive
- ▸▸ To create a forced error or winner
- ▸▸ To win the physical battle
- ▸▸ To create an opportunity to win the point

  (Any of the same three opportunities from working the point)
  A fourth opportunity may present itself—a ball that floats back
  defensively. This opportunity will occur when the player has
  intended to hit a good shot, but has actually produced a great
  shot. It also occurs when his opponent is late arriving to the ball
  and is forced to extend his arm and must hit a defensive shot.
  The player must be alert in both situations to take advantage of
  floating shots by moving toward the net and volleying the ball into
  the open corner with a good angle.

A simplified version of the thought process involved in constructing a point
is shown in Figure 5. The player either works the point or dictates the point
and looks for an opportunity which will then lead to an option.

FIGURE 5

Constructing A Point
Two Approaches

THE OPTIONS

Once an opportunity presents itself, the player has four options to consider.

Option #1—He can be patient and continue what he is doing because:

a he simply chooses to outsteady his opponent (and looks for the unforced error or forced error)

b he has the feeling (maybe due to nerves) it is not time to make a more aggressive move and will wait for a better opportunity, such as an even shorter ball (better proximity) or even slower ball to occur later in the point

c he is in low intensity and lacks confidence to be more aggressive.

Option #2 He chooses to hit a more aggressive shot (more pace, more depth, or better angle) because:

a he is gaining momentum and confidence and feels comfortable taking the risk to force an error

b he wants to force his opponent into providing him with a better opportunity, which is defined as an even shorter or slower paced ball.

Either option #1 or option #2 could lead to a better opportunity. Once the player gets the shot he wants, he will attempt to force his opponent into an error or choose to finish the point with option #3 or #4.

Option #3 He chooses to go for a winner

An aggressive option is to try to end the point by hitting a winner. A smart player will only go for high-percentage winners. He should ask himself: Can I hit a high-percentage shot off the pace of his oncoming ball? What is the height of the bounce—is it good for the shot I want to hit? Will I hit from a favorable position on the court? It would also be favorable if his opponent is out of position. Many players make a mental error here because they think hitting a winner is always the best option. *Just because the opportunity is there does not always mean it is the smart shot to hit.* Hitting winners requires effective timing, good margins, and a high level of concentration. The player places more pressure on himself when he attempts to hit a winner instead of an approach shot. He needs to be sure before going for broke!

Option #4 He chooses to attack the net

Another aggressive option would be to attack the net. Attacking the net is the most aggressive component of baseline point development because it provides the greatest challenge and applies the most pressure on all of his opponent's physical and mental abilities (speed, footwork, hands, concentration, and timing). In addition, *passing shots are the most difficult shots to execute under pressure.* Attacking the net is a proactive move and forces his opponent to be reactive in hitting passing shots and lobs. The player will use the same basic weapons—spin, pace, depth, and angle—to gain the same advantages as he did on the baseline. The closer he gets to the net, the more effective his angles can be. Underspin on the approach shot and volley also keep the ball low, making it take a quick second bounce, and forcing an opponent to hit up to the player at the net.

SET-UP SHOT

Attacking the net involves a two-step sequence of shots: the set-up shot and the finish shot. *The first key to a successful attack is to hit a well placed approach as the set-up shot.* The player can hit an underspin approach shot or a well hit, angled topspin groundstroke to the corner and attack the net. Whichever shot he chooses, it should be hit with enough pace to challenge his opponent's timing yet allow himself sufficient time to move into a good volley position at the net. The smartest play is usually down the line because such a shot gets him into the best volley position. He will also be placing his opponent in a vulnerable position. A crosscourt approach shot is a low-percentage choice because the player will take more steps to get into a good position and will not have enough time to cover his opponent's down-the-line passing shot. As a general rule, he should only hit crosscourt if he is going for a winner. The exception to this rule: If a cross-court ball forces his opponent to play a down-the-line passing shot he doesn't have the confidence to hit, then the player should attempt the crosscourt approach or wait for a better opportunity.

When his opponent's shot lands in the middle of the court, the player has the choice of hitting his approach to either corner. He should choose the corner where his opponent has had more trouble with his passing shots during the match.

The second key to success in attacking the net is to establish good position. A player must establish his position and be balanced before his opponent strikes the ball. The smart player uses the "possible returns" as a guide for good positioning. This mental exercise analyzes the best passing shot his opponent can hit to the player's forehand side and also to his backhand side. These two angled shots form a **V** from where his opponent is positioned on the court (see

FIGURE 6
Possible Returns

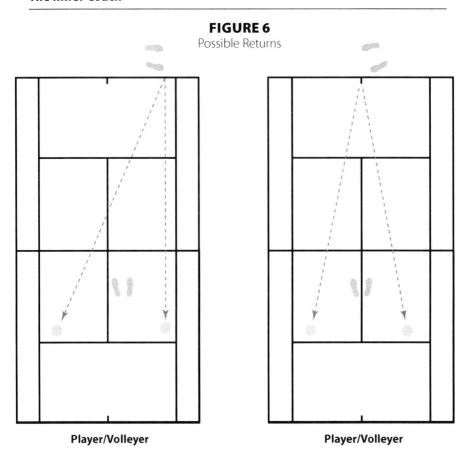

Player/Volleyer   Player/Volleyer

Figure 6). The player positions himself in the center of the two angles so he has an equal distance to reach either passing shot. He now has taken the best position to make a play.

FINISH SHOT

The player counts on his set-up shot and effective position to lead to the opportunity to end the point with a finish shot, such as an overhead smash, a hard-angled volley, or a drop volley. *Many players make the mistake of thinking the finish shot has to be a winner.* They commit many unnecessary errors with this philosophy like over hitting or playing shots with little margin for error. Smart players win points on both forced errors and winners, so why risk the low-percentage winner?

A player also might miss a shot if he lacks a target, has the wrong target in mind, or fails to use self-coaching techniques. He should remind himself to add good margin to the finish shot. And there is always the possibility that his

FIGURE 7
Two Approaches

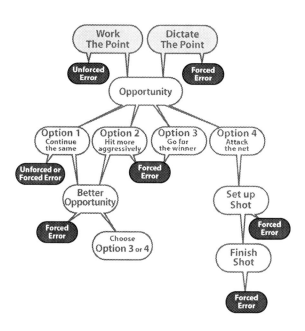

opponent will neutralize his attempted finish shot. If that happens, the player must be patient and continue his development of the point. The smart player anticipates this possibility and is always ready to follow up with one or two more good shots to finish a point.

A more complete version of the thought process involved in the two approaches to baseline groundstroke point development is shown in Figure 7.

After countless hours of practice matches and actual competition, the player will learn to follow the flow of either approach with such ease that it will seem like second nature.

COMBINATION APPROACH

At times the player will find it useful to *combine* the two approaches to groundstroke point development. In this combination approach, the player wants to get in the flow of the point by starting with the steady, conservative method of *working the point*. He is trying for an unforced error, but if that does not occur after several (five or six) shots, the player looks for an opportunity to take control of the point. As soon as he gets a shorter or slower ball, the player moves into the more aggressive mode of *dictating the point.*

Once again, the player tries to create an opportunity (a ball he can hit with his best shot, a ball that floats back defensively…), which will present him with the choice of four options. The same information provided earlier concerning the options applies here as well for the player. (See Figure 8)

Situations when the player should use the combination approach include:

- ▶▶ Critical points in the game (begin with working the point)
- ▶▶ Critical points in the match (begin with working the point)
- ▶▶ When the player is behind in the score but is playing with good intensity.

Figure 8 below provides a detailed sketch of the flow of the combination approach.

FIGURE 8
Combination Approach

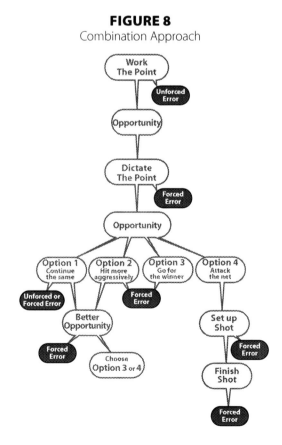

The player must be adept at all the approaches to baseline groundstroke point development if he is to be successful at a high level of play. As he becomes more skilled, he will know intuitively which approach to use in any given point, and will feel comfortable either working the point or dictating the point, as the situation on court requires.

DEFENDING AGAINST AGGRESSIVE PLAY

There are times when his opponent chooses to be the aggressor and attacks the net. He has to decide whether to hit a passing shot or a lob. His decision is determined by how well his opponent has hit his shot. If his opponent has hit his shot extremely well, the highest percentage shot would be a defensive lob. The smart player knows if he hits a successful lob over his opponent's head and has him retreating, he should move just inside his service line so he can take advantage of a potential weak return. He also knows if he hits an effective lob that forces his opponent to hit a weak overhead, he wants to go on the offensive and force his opponent to play defensively. This switch from offense to defense is a very difficult transition to make mentally.

If a player likes the ball he has to hit and sees a good shot, he will have to choose between hitting a passing shot or a topspin lob. He has two choices for his passing shot if that is what he chooses. He can go for an aggressive passing shot right away or he can play more conservatively by hitting his first passing shot to place his opponent in a vulnerable position near the singles sideline (Shot A). Then he can try to hit a winner with his second passing shot to the open court (Shot C—see Figure 9). The player does not have to hit an aggressive shot if his opponent has not attained a good net position. The score also matters. *When a player is losing or down in a game, he will want to add margin to his shot to ensure it will stay in play to create additional pressure on his opponent's shot.*

SERVING AND VOLLEYING

A serve-and-volley player will begin to work toward taking control of the point with his first serve. His first volley should be a set-up shot unless he has a high percentage shot he can hit for a winner. In Figure 10, note that the server's first volley should go to either **V1** or **V2** to place his opponent in a vulnerable position. Which corner he chooses will depend on the placement of the serve. The server has three good options for each serve.

In the add court, Serve 1 (**S1**) draws his opponent toward the center of the court to make the return. As a result, the server has the choice of going to either corner with his volley. He can hit to **V1** either to make his opponent run farther, or to play to his opponent's weaker side (if this side has been noticeably weaker in earlier points). Or, he could hit his first volley to **V2** to hit behind his opponent. Serve 2 (**S2**) will draw his opponent into the doubles alley for the return. The player should volley to **V1** to make his opponent run across the court to reach the ball. Serve 3 (**S3**) will jam his opponent and force more of a defensive return. Again, the player should hit to **V1** to run his opponent the farthest distance. When serving **S1**, **S2**, and **S3** in the deuce court, the first volleys will be just the opposite i.e., reverse **V1** and **V2**.

FIGURE 9
Passing Shots
2-SHOT SEQUENCES

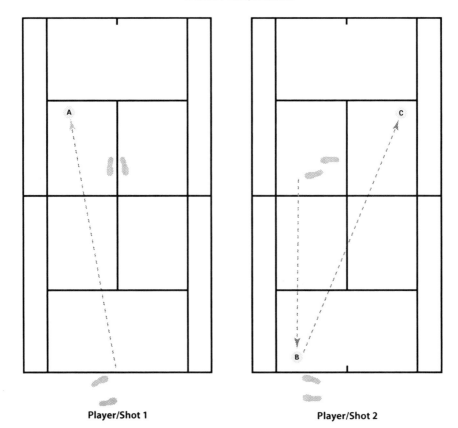

Player/Shot 1   Player/Shot 2

FIGURE 10
Service And First-Volley Options

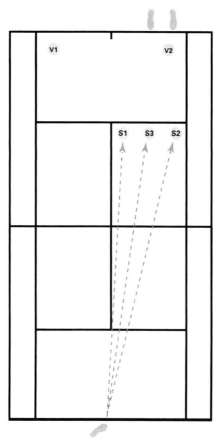

Server

The serve-and-volley player can then angle his second volley to the opposite corner. This will force his opponent to hit another passing shot or the lob on the run. The server should continue to hit volleys and overheads to opposite corners until he forces an error or can end the point. He must be careful not to give his opponent too many chances to pass him because *the likelihood of success increases with each attempt.* A good volleyer should end the point with the second or third volley.

RETURNING SERVE

The player can also start his point development when he is returning serve. Against an opponent who stays on the baseline, a conservative return would be to hit to the middle of the backcourt halfway between the center and the corner. There is little risk with this shot, and it puts an opponent slightly on the run. A more aggressive return would be to one of the corners. This places his opponent immediately in a vulnerable position and the player may have a chance to start dictating the point. This riskier return is better suited to a player who is ahead in the score and playing at a high level of intensity.

FIGURE 11
Off-Center Return Of Serve

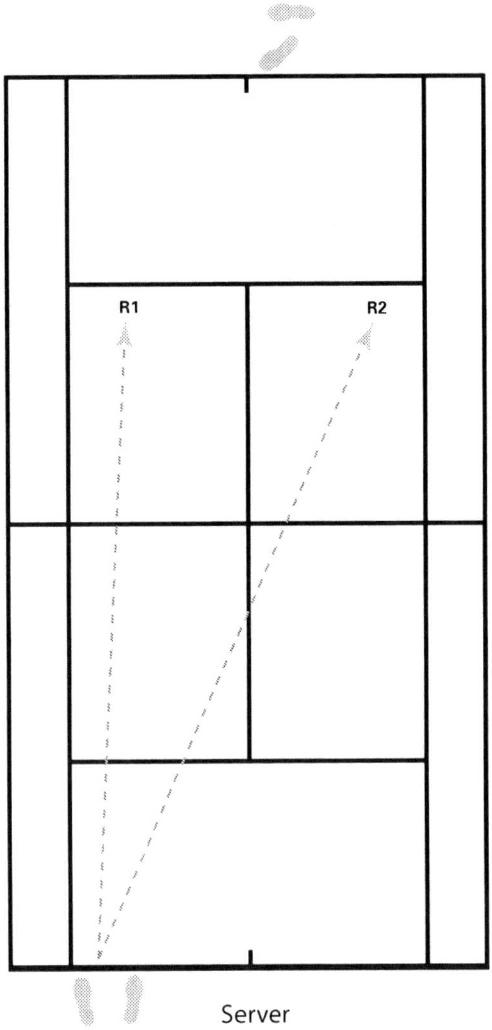

Server

DEFENDING THE SERVE-AND-VOLLEY

The player returning against a serve-and-volley opponent has several good options. One choice is to hit a shot over the center strap below an opponent's knees. This forces an opponent to contend with the net on his volley or half volley. It may also require he take some pace off his shot compared to a volley hit above the net. The disadvantage of this return is that his opponent remains in a centered position for the next shot.

In Figure 11, both Return 1 (**R1**) and Return 2 (**R2**) are good choices, and are even better if his opponent is forced to hit the first volley below net level. **R2** is similar to hitting a good crosscourt doubles return which is very effective against the serve and volley opponent. With both **R1** and **R2**, the server is forced off center for the first volley, which leaves an open court and makes him vulnerable. The player should now hit his opponent's first volley to the open court to increase his vulnerability, force an error, or win the point outright. The player increases his chances of winning the point as he increases the distance his opponent has to move for each volley.

The smart player is confident in his ability to develop points to reach a high level of play. He considers both the timing of his shot selection and which approach is best for the situation. After playing countless practice and competitive matches, he will develop a "natural feel" for the timing and the choices he has available. He will gain experience and confidence in his point development and will learn how to play a smart point.

Dave (third from left) helped lead his Indiana University team to the Big Ten title in 1964.

Junior Davis Cuppers

From left to right: Jim Buck, captain; Bill Harris; Bob Lutz; Stan Smith; James Beste; Jerry Cromwell; Dave Power; George Seewagen. Not present when picture was taken: John Pickens.

As a member of the 1964 Junior Davis Cup Squad, Dave competed against the top national and international players.

Dave (far left) played exhibitions in eight countries, including Ethiopia (shown here) on a 1967 Goodwill Tour for the U.S. State Department.

As part of the Goodwill Tour, Dave and his teammates also put on a clinic for young players in Southeast Asia.

In 1967, Dave (far left) played on the USTA overseas team to Australia with Arthur Ashe (third from left).

Billie Jean King (far right) visited with Dave's nationally ranked players during a tour stop in Cincinnati in 1979.

Dave interviewed top players including Michael Chang for a cable network at the Cincinnati ATP Tour stop in the early '90s.

1986, Dave with former student Caroline Kuhlman, National Junior Champion and qualifier for U.S. Open.

In 2006, Dave was inducted into the Indiana University Athletic Hall of Fame along with fellow inductees including Dick Enberg.

Since 1997, Dave has coached top junior players at the
Windward Tennis Academy in Alpharetta, Ga.

7

Patterns of Play

THE ABILITY TO RECOGNIZE AND TO DEVELOP PATTERNS IS AN IMPORTANT part of constructing a point. Patterns can help a player detect weaknesses in his opponent's game and can also be used to surprise him. As often as possible in a match players should try to outsmart their opponents with unexpected shots. When that happens, who doesn't get a little frustrated and lose confidence?

The potential for a pattern begins when a player hits a particular shot successfully. The pattern develops when he chooses to hit the identical shot the next time a similar circumstance comes up. He continues to use that pattern until he thinks he needs to change it to win the point. The use of patterns helps to keep his opponent off-balance and guessing.

ESTABLISHING A PATTERN

The smart player can develop a pattern with any stroke and realizes he always has several options to respond to any shot his opponent throws at him. For instance, the player can develop a pattern as his opponent hits an approach shot to his forehand corner. He can hit a passing shot crosscourt and win the point. A few points or games later, when his opponent comes to the net on a similar approach, he can respond with another crosscourt passing shot. The player has now established a successful pattern and has set a "trap" for his opponent. His opponent, however, is very upset with himself for allowing the player to beat him twice with the same shot. He knows he cannot afford to let the player continue to beat him in such a way, and so he will anticipate that shot the next time the same situation occurs.

The player now needs to make a decision. He can keep hitting the same shot, or he can change the pattern. If his opponent has not been very successful in defending against the shot and the player believes he has a good chance of winning again with it, he should continue to hit the same shot. However, if his opponent has anticipated the shot, or put a racquet on the ball and has come close to winning the point, or even taken a better net position, then it would be time to change the pattern. In this way, the player is able to frustrate his opponent and to stay one step ahead of him.

BREAKING A PATTERN

If the player believes that the time is right to break the pattern, the next time his opponent approaches to his forehand corner, he can attempt to pass him with a down-the-line shot. This should be relatively easy to accomplish because his opponent will be guarding against the crosscourt passing shot and he might not react quickly enough to an unexpected shot. His opponent has now fallen into the player's trap and has been beaten with two different shots. This is a very important factor in the match, for once the player has established two different shots that win, his opponent has a much harder time defending against those shots. *His opponent can no longer afford to overplay either shot;* that is, he cannot take away one shot by moving his body closer to the side to which he thinks the ball will be hit. With two shots used effectively against him, his opponent now has to anticipate which one will be hit, and hope that he is right most of the time.

A player needs to develop shots in pairs, such as the crosscourt passing shot and the down-the-line passing shot, because each shot individually then becomes much more effective (as proven above). However the next time the same situation occurs, the player can use a third choice, the lob, to frustrate his opponent who will be mentally vulnerable to the lob. His opponent will be expecting a passing shot, for that is all he has been beaten with so far in the match. Now, the player has won with three options, and is dominating that segment of play. *It is important for the player to realize it is in his best interest to try all of his shot options to probe his opponent's game for weaknesses.*

Once the player has used all three options, there is no longer an element of surprise at his disposal. However, continuing to alternate his options will keep his opponent off balance. His opponent may choose not to continue coming to net. He may also start to feel frustrated and even feel that he is over-matched.

STROKE PATTERNS

WRONG-FOOTING

A good baseline ground stroke pattern is wrong-footing, or hitting behind, an opponent. The player sets up the pattern by hitting every shot to an opposite corner. If a player starts to win points in this manner, his opponent knows he must try to defend the open corner better. Knowing that the player always hits the ball consistently to the open corner, he is forced to move faster to defend that corner. Before long, his opponent gets wrong-footed when the pattern is broken.

The smart player knows when the opportunity is there for him by watching his opponent's feet. He wants to make sure his opponent's feet are moving so quickly that he will not be able to change direction easily. He looks to see when his opponent is within three or four feet of the center of the baseline. Then he breaks the pattern and hits his shot right back where he hit the last ball. It's usually a winner.

SERVICE PATTERNS

Smart players save the best surprises for the biggest points. For instance, when the player is serving, he could set a pattern by hitting a flat first serve down the middle on the first point of his first two service games. On the first point of the third game his opponent will be looking for that same serve down the middle. The player changes the pattern by hitting a slice first serve out wide which catches his opponent off guard. Having established both serves, he can now use them effectively in his point development. He saves his third option, serving directly at his opponent, for a critical point at the end of the first set when he can surprise his opponent with it.

The same pattern can unfold within the same game. In the above example, the player could also hit his flat first serve down the middle when serving his first two points to the deuce court. The third time he serves his first serve to the deuce court, he decides to change the pattern by hitting a slice out wide.

SERVICE RETURNS

The player can establish a pattern on the first two points of the return of serve in a similar way. Regardless of where his opponent serves, the player might hit his return to his opponent's backhand corner. He now has set the pattern and looks for a serve he can hit with a high percentage shot to his opponent's forehand corner to change the pattern. He may even surprise his opponent by hitting the ball hard right down the center of the court. The player could reverse this pattern by hitting the first two returns right down the center of the court and the third return to one of the corners.

THE IMPORTANCE OF PATTERNS

If the player is having trouble during a match with one of his options, his game becomes more limited and much easier to defend against. The player who has only one option, or is only hitting one option well during the match, will struggle to win points because he is now very predictable. A player in a low intensity level will have trouble setting up patterns because his strokes are too inconsistent to do so. But once he is able to raise his intensity level and make the shots necessary to keep all his options alive, he will be capable of setting up patterns.

The player will need to develop and change patterns throughout the match. He must keep his intensity level high so that he might have a pattern in some stage of development in every game. *It is even possible for him to have several patterns evolving in the same game.* For instance, he may be setting up a pattern by serving in the deuce court to a particular spot, and in the same game he may choose to break the pattern he had been using on his approach shot.

DEFENDING AGAINST PATTERNS

While developing points, the player also must be able to defend against his opponent's use of patterns. The player must discover how many shots his opponent is able to hit successfully, so he will know how many options his opponent has in his patterns. He needs to learn his opponent's tendencies in certain situations that will make his shots more predictable. *The player must learn quickly which option his opponent hits best and take that away from him.* His opponent now will have to win with his second or third best option which will be easier to defend against.

The easiest opponent to play is the one who always hits the same shots in the same situations, or only has one weapon in his arsenal. This shot becomes predictable and easily defended. However, an opponent with two or more strong options is more difficult to defend against.

USING REMINDERS

If his opponent has proven that he can be successful with more than one shot option, a player's defense becomes more complicated. For every shot, the player must cover all three options, both mentally and physically. Two of the options are covered by physical position on the court and the third is covered mentally through the use of a reminder. For example, a player centered on the baseline can cover physically the shots to the corners, but is vulnerable to the drop shot or the short shot which he needs to cover mentally. If his opponent hits a short ball, the player will be able to read and react to it more quickly because he has anticipated it. Another example: if the player is at the net in a good volley position, he is prepared physically for the two passing shots, but is vulnerable to the lob. Therefore, he must cover mentally the possibility of a lob by using a reminder (watch for the lob). *As a rule, a player should always cover the shot mentally to which he is vulnerable as a result of his physical position.* If the player positions himself further off the net to offset his opponent's good lobbing ability, then he has to prepare himself mentally for the passing shots. He must remind himself to move in quickly once he reads the passing shot that has been hit. The player who is conscientious in covering mentally and physically all three options will provide an effective defense.

Whenever a player finds himself in a vulnerable position, he can use reminders to defend himself. For example, when he is moving in toward the net so quickly for a volley that it would be very difficult to stop his momentum and change direction, he should remind himself about a lob. Or, if he is in one corner and starts moving quickly across the baseline in anticipation of the ball being hit to the opposite corner, he needs to remind himself of the possibility of getting wrong-footed. If he is anticipating it, the player will respond better and defend more effectively against that shot. The smart player will combine his physical and mental abilities in an ongoing effort to be successful when he becomes vulnerable.

THE IMPORTANCE OF CREATIVITY

Creativity plays a significant role in the player's use of patterns. He must be resourceful in setting up and developing his patterns by choosing which shots to use and when to use them. The player must consider the different choices he has on each ball he hits, and decide how to blend those options in his developing patterns. He must take into account the court position of his opponent and his own position, and then choose the shots that are most likely to succeed. The player must be able to sense when he has hooked his opponent with his pattern, and then decide the precise time to change it. This will help him to maximize the number of points he wins with his use of patterns. The creative player will do the unexpected as he mentally outmaneuvers his opponent through his innovative use of patterns.

Patterns will create doubt, confusion and uncertainty. In a close match, sometimes patterns are the only edge a player has. He needs to exploit them. Developing creative patterns that suit his game and capabilities, then using them in practice and in matches, will help them become a regular part of his game.

8

Match Tactics

THE EFFECTIVE USE OF TACTICS REFLECTS THE DEPTH OF A PLAYER'S MENTAL game and plays an important role in his game plan. Tactics are ploys used skillfully by the player who is attempting to gain an edge in a particular point. A tactic executed successfully at the right time can make the difference in a critical game and become the turning point in a match. A successful tactic can be repeated often enough to make the difference in the outcome of the match.

The role of tactics is three-fold. They are used to exploit the opponent's weaknesses; to surprise him by catching him off-guard and disrupting his rhythm; and, to negate his strengths.

EXPLOITING THE OPPONENT'S WEAKNESSES

Once the player figures out how to take advantage of an opponent's weakness, he should begin to use that tactic continuously. For example:

1 The player recognizes his opponent cannot hurt him with pace or accuracy on passing shots from his forehand side so he continuously hits his approach shots to the forehand side.

2 The opponent's backhand volley is much weaker than his forehand volley so the player hits all his passing shots to the backhand side. He may even choose to bring him in to the net more often to take advantage of this weakness.

3 The opponent has a weak overhead so the player continuously lobs rather than hit passing shots.

4 The opponent over-hits his approach shots, so the player hits more short balls or drop shots to force him into repeated mistakes.

5 The opponent has a weak backhand return of serve. The player wants to make it more difficult for him to run around his backhand. So, he changes his service position on the baseline which allows him to deliver a better angle into his backhand corner and *forces* his opponent to hit the backhand return. If he shifts over too far toward the alley, the player hits a flat serve down the middle.

The smart player understands that any tactic he uses too often has the potential to lose its effectiveness. If he stops winning a majority of the points, he needs to vary his shot placements to challenge his opponent's timing and keep him off-balance.

SURPRISING THE OPPONENT

The use of tactics can also keep an opponent on edge and disrupt his rhythm. A smart player wants to make his opponent more reactive. To accomplish this, the player should mix up his shots frequently, and then choose the right time in a match to pull off a surprising shot. Confident players will do this when they need to win a critical point in a crucial game. A few tactics that might surprise an opponent are:

THE SURPRISE SERVE AND VOLLEY. This is a good play for a player who hasn't come in off his serve much in a match. It can be used whenever a player observes his opponent starting to hit returns more conservatively—five or six feet over the net with little pace.

THE SURPRISE CHIP AND CHARGE. Again, this works best if a player has stayed on the baseline after returning serve throughout most of the match. This tactic forces the opposing server to hit a passing shot when he might not be prepared to do so. This is a good ploy when the game score is 15–30, 15–40, and on ad points, especially in critical games or in tiebreaks.

THE SURPRISE MID-POINT ATTACK. A player should do this occasionally after hitting an aggressive groundstroke during a baseline rally. Normally, he would avoid doing this because it would leave him in a poor position to volley. But in this situation, his opponent will often be so surprised that he will send back a weak reply, which a player can capitalize on.

THE FAKE NET RUSH. A player takes a few quick steps toward the net after his first serve to give the appearance of serving and volleying, but instead retreats quickly to the baseline for the rally. The player is hoping his opponent will become distracted by the movement and take his eye off the ball. His opponent might lose his rhythm, or try to hit a better return than he needs to.

THE COUNTER-VOLLEY. If an opponent has been serving and volleying on his second serve, the player can chip and charge on his return to place more pressure on his opponent's first volley. Not only will his opponent have less time to prepare for the shot, he will also be forced to hit a more accurate volley.

THE CHANGE-UP. A player can choose to hit his second serve as a first serve. If he normally hits a flat first serve and a spin second serve, he would hit his spin second serve as his first serve. He could even serve and volley off this serve. The slower serve would allow him to get into a position closer to the net for his first volley. He could also choose to hit his flat first serve at more of a second serve speed to throw off the timing of his opponent who is expecting a faster serve.

THE SURPRISE FIRST SERVE. After missing a first serve, a player might occasionally serve his second serve at first serve speed. This is a risky ploy and should not be attempted on a critical point. But if the player is confident, serving well, and has a cushion in the score, he should consider this tactic.

NEGATING THE OPPONENT'S STRENGTHS

A smart player will self-coach with tactics like changing his position on the court or changing the location of his shots to try to negate the strengths of his opponent. A position change usually involves some type of trade off. The player gains something he needs, but in doing so creates a vulnerability for himself. A greater gain must be achieved for the tactic to be successful. Sometimes the only gain is disrupting his opponent's rhythm.

Some changes in position a player can use to throw off an opponent's timing or rhythm are:

➤➤ The player can return serve a couple of steps inside the baseline. By playing closer in, he not only reduces his opponent's angles, but might challenge his opponent to hit a bigger serve. This could throw his timing off. The player realizes this ploy makes him vulnerable to a big hard serve, so he will only do it when his opponent's serve is weak or to neutralize an effective serve out wide.

▸▸ A smart player sometimes might return serve several steps behind the baseline. By playing further back, the player will have more time to read and react to the serve. This gives him more time for his backswing, which allows him to take a big cut. This tactic can negate a strong server. The player needs to be careful because with this tactic he becomes more vulnerable to a serve out wide.

▸▸ The player can take his position before his opponent starts to serve, or begin moving from his normal position to the new return-of-serve spot as his opponent begins his service preparation. The player can remain in the new position or he can return to his original position as his opponent starts his service motion. If he chooses to return to his old spot, his motive was not to take advantage of the new position, but rather to get in his opponent's head.

▸▸ The player can change his position two to three feet from where he typically stands to defend against his opponent's strength or to protect a weakness. Moving his position will make it harder for his opponent to hit an effective shot to his weakness. It will also make it easier for the player to run around his weakness and hit the shot with his stronger stroke. A player can do this during baseline rallies, to defend more effectively against big serves, and to guard against a specific passing shot.

▸▸ Another smart shift in position occurs when the player wants to show a greater opening on one side of the court in the hopes that his opponent will see this opening and hit his shot there. The player will then move to cover the open court just as his opponent has committed to his shot and starts his forward swing to strike the ball. This is a good tactic to use when the player is vulnerable after hitting a short volley. He knows he will have less reaction time so he attempts to reduce his opponent's options by shifting his position.

▸▸ Sometimes a player can benefit by changing his position for no particular reason. Trying something different is a proactive move and may be just what is needed to pick him up if he isn't playing well.

CHANGING SHOT PLACEMENT

Some ideas for how to mix up shot placement to negate an opponent's strength include:

ATTACK THE MIDDLE. A good tactic against an opponent who is hitting accurate passing shots from both corners is to hit the approach shot down the center of the court. The player has now reduced the angles his opponent can hit on his passing shots.

APPROACH OFF A SHORT BALL. Instead of hitting an approach shot deep, the player should hit it so it bounces just inside the service line and forces his opponent to hit his passing shot from a few feet behind the service line. This tactic forces his opponent to move to the ball on an angle. It also changes the angles available to him on his passing shot. Players rarely attempt their passing shots from this position on the court, so they will probably not be as comfortable hitting from here. This tactic also works well against an opponent who lobs well from the baseline. It forces him to lob from a different position on the court.

HIT RIGHT AT HIM. When an opponent is hitting his volleys well and anticipating well, the player should consider hitting a passing shot directly at him to catch him off guard. The next time he comes to the net, he might freeze his position for a split second. This would be a good tactic against a tall opponent with long arms who has good reach for wide volleys because it takes away his strength in covering wide shots.

The effective use of a variety of tactics can make the difference in a close match. The smart player looks for opportunities to use these ploys in each of his matches. If he practices, for example, shifting his position on the court to hit some of his shots; changing the placement of his shots; and adding new shots to his repertoire that might surprise his opponent, he will soon have a better understanding of how these tactics (and others) can affect the match.

9

Self-Coaching

Tennis is one of the few sports where a player becomes his own coach during competition. Because there is minimal or no coaching allowed during matches, the player must learn how to evaluate all aspects of his game. A smart player learns quickly to depend upon himself to find a way to win matches even when he is not playing at the top of his game. If his timing is off on his best stroke, or if he is just having a bad day, the player who develops self-coaching techniques for every aspect of his game is the one who will reach his potential at a high level of competitive play. The more comprehensive his self-coaching system, the fewer unforced errors the player will commit. The smart player will know how to use reminders continuously to avoid making mental errors throughout his match.

Self-coaching helps the player maintain a higher level of concentration during and between points. *The player who is skilled at self-coaching is involved in a constant process of assessment and decision-making during the entire match.* Whether he is winning or losing, he uses self-coaching as he analyzes different situations and makes decisions that affect what he is accomplishing on the court. The player knows how to protect a lead, and also how to attack problems once they occur.

Obviously, there is a greater need to self-coach when the player is losing; however, a lead can evaporate suddenly and he must be able to recognize and correct a problem as soon as possible. The sooner he detects a problem, the more promptly he can correct it so future points will not be jeopardized.

If a player needs to correct a problem, there are three steps he must follow in the self-coaching process:

1 He must analyze the situation and identify the problem.

2 He must make the proper adjustment to correct it.

3 He must monitor the adjustment to make sure the problem does not arise again.

The player can apply this process to every stroke, margin, and tactic he uses in his game.

SELF-ANALYSIS

In order to prevent or deal with stroke errors, every player needs to learn the basic fundamentals that make up each of his strokes. For example, on his forehand or backhand, he must be aware of the grip he uses, the backswing, the angle of the forward swing, the position of the racquet head at contact, the distance from his body contact is made, and the proper follow-through for the shot. Hitting hundreds of balls with a particular stroke helps teach what makes up a good stroke and what creates errors.

Stroke errors are the result of a breakdown in basic technique. For example, a player may pull his racquet too quickly across his body during his follow through on a groundstroke. This may cause him to lose his timing.

The player who makes the same error several times over a short period must determine if there is a pattern to the mistakes he is making. For example, suppose he realizes that he has been hitting the ball late on his forehand. He needs to understand what type(s) of error he is committing on this shot:

A STROKE ERROR. Perhaps his mechanics are just off. This could be because he is taking too big of a backswing in relation to the pace of an incoming ball.

INCORRECT READING OF THE BALL. This can happen when a player does not read the pace of the ball correctly, so it arrives sooner than expected and he hits late.

POOR FOOTWORK. The player might not be moving well that day, so he gets to the ball late, resulting in late contact.

MAKING ADJUSTMENTS

Once the player determines which problem is causing him to hit late, he can make the appropriate adjustment:

▸▸ **FOR A STROKE ERROR**, his adjustment would be either to shorten his backswing, or to start his backswing earlier;

▸▸ **FOR A PROBLEM READING THE BALL**, the player must start picking up the ball more quickly off his opponent's racquet and must pay more attention to the pace and spin of the oncoming ball;

▸▸ **THE FOOTWORK ERROR** might be remedied by a quicker first step and some additional hustle.

Once an adjustment is made, he must monitor the change to make sure the problem has been corrected. If the adjustment he chooses does not provide an adequate solution, he must find another way to correct the problem. He has self-coached well if he no longer hits the ball late.

GOING TO THE OPPOSITE EXTREME

To remedy a faulty stroke, there are self-coaching stroke adjustment techniques a player can use. The first technique is called "going to the opposite extreme." This can be utilized when he is struggling with a particular shot that is going continuously short or long. For instance, if his forehand shots are landing short, he should strive to hit his next shot or two beyond the baseline. That is going to the opposite extreme and can help correct a problem.

Once he misses long a couple of times, he can ease up on the pace it took to hit a deeper shot, or lower the clearance over the net slightly, and the ball should land inside the baseline. With this self-coaching technique, he may lose a few points as he tries to over-hit, but once he finds his range he will save many future points.

Going to the opposite extreme can also be useful for balls that are going long. First, the player has to determine if he has enough topspin on the ball for the pace at which he is hitting. If not, the appropriate adjustment would be to add more topspin and see if that corrects the problem. If he increases the topspin and the ball still goes long, he should then hit with less pace and/or reduce the clearance of the ball over the net until the ball lands either where he wants it to, or shorter than he wishes. He may even have to aim his shot for the headband (the top of the net) to be successful.

Once the ball lands in the desired location, he has to recall both the pace at which he hit the ball, and the clearance of the ball over the net so he can continue to be successful with that shot. If it lands too short (such as just outside of the service box), he has gone to the opposite extreme. Now he will have to increase the pace of the ball slightly and/or increase the clearance over the net to achieve the desired location.

ADJUSTING TARGETS

A second self-coaching adjustment is a target adjustment. A good player has control of his shots and usually is able to hit near a target that he sets, such as within four feet of the sideline on every shot. However, if his timing is off this will be difficult to accomplish, and the player will need to make an adjustment to hit his intended target.

In Figure 12, the player's target for a particular shot is **A**, but he makes an error as his shot lands instead at **B**. The player must measure mentally the distance from **A** to **B** to know how much of an adjustment is necessary. If he perceives the distance he is missing his target to be four feet to the right of **A**, then he must make his new target **C**, four feet to the left of **A**. Although the player will strive to hit the ball to location **C**, he hopes that by adjusting his target and aiming toward **C**, the ball will land closer to **A**. If it does not, he should move his target further to the left with his next shot. He knows his timing is back when he can aim for **A** and actually hit the ball to **A**.

REMINDERS

Another aspect of self-coaching is the use of positive reminders. A reminder is a mental message that the player uses to remember what he needs to do on the next shot, point, or game. A reminder can consist of as little as one or two words, or it can be a complete sentence. A good player will be providing himself with reminders constantly to help prevent errors. Many players have not developed this aspect of self-coaching fully enough. Some players let negative thoughts creep in, which can be very damaging to their games. For instance, if the player misses the first serve and then begins to think about the possibility of a double fault, it is very likely that he *will* double fault. *The player should replace this negative thought with a positive reminder:* Place the toss in a good location, and visualize good hand movement for better ball control.

Some other reminders that can help are:

FIGURE 12
Target Adjustment

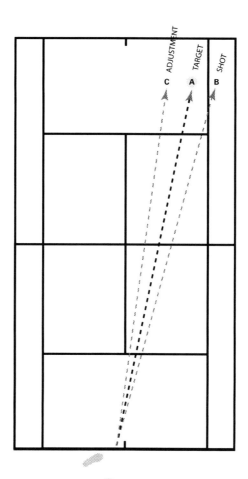

▶▶ When his opponent shows signs of fatigue, the player should remind himself to hit a wide serve so his opponent has to exert a quick burst of energy.

▶▶ After hitting a groundstroke into the net, a player should remind himself to hit higher over the net or hit more shots crosscourt to take advantage of the lowest part of the net.

▶▶ When taking his eye off the ball and mis-hitting it, he should remind himself to track the ball closer in to the contact point.

▶▶ When his opponent is unable to get to the player's next shot, he should remind himself just to keep the ball in play with a conservative shot.

▸▸ When serving and volleying in a crucial point, the player should consider the two toughest returns his opponent can hit and be prepared to handle both.

▸▸ When a ball gets too low to hit an overhead, he should remind himself to hit a high forehand volley.

PREVENTING MENTAL ERRORS

Much of the discussion thus far has centered on forced and unforced errors. Mental errors, however, also can affect the player's game and cost him points, often at critical times in the match.

A few mental errors to watch for are:

FORGETTING THE SCORE. A player must not only remember the score, but he must be able to recall every point in the order that it was played in case there is a scoring dispute. Saying the score before each point is played helps to avoid this problem.

STARTING THE MATCH TOO SOON. Smart players use all their warm-up time properly. Matches are often lost due to lack of proper preparation.

REPEATING AN ERROR. Making the same error on consecutive shots may sound like an unforced error, but it is really a mental error. Make the proper adjustment to avoid repeating the same error. Smart players do not make the same error twice in a row.

SECOND-GUESSING. The player should stay with his first instinct. He will make more errors when he is indecisive.

GETTING CHEATED AND DOING NOTHING. At the very least, the player must question his opponent's call if he was sure his shot was good. This sends the message that the player is competing and his opponent must be fair in his future calls.

BEING STUBBORN. Staying with a shot that is not working. A shot needs to be effective a minimum of 50% of the time to stay with it, or cease using it.

PREVENTING PHYSICAL ERRORS

A few physical problems a player must guard against in two key areas of the game concern footwork and the serve.

FOOTWORK

MOVING TOO EARLY. This happens when a player starts to move in anticipation of the next shot before finishing the follow-through of the present shot. He must concentrate on the present shot before moving for the next shot.

HITTING ON THE RUN. Sometimes players hit the ball on the run when they have time to stop and set their feet. Timing is more difficult when the body is still moving as contact is made. He must stop and set his feet.

OVERRUNNING THE BALL. This can be corrected by taking shorter steps as the player approaches the ball to avoid letting the ball get too close to the body. *It could also be due to an improper read of the ball.*

HITTING SHOTS OFF-BALANCE. This happens when a player is unable to stop his momentum and continues to take an extra step or two after contacting the ball. This places the player farther out of position for the next shot and also forces him to run a greater distance. To fix this problem, a player should practice taking shorter steps as he approaches each shot.

SERVING

DOUBLE-FAULTING TWICE IN A ROW. This can be avoided by planning to hit two second serves after the first double-fault. There can be transfer of information if both serves are the same (both spin). The player would also be able to make an adjustment from the missed second serve of the last point.

HITTING A SECOND SERVE TOO QUICKLY. The player needs to take his time and make sure he is mentally ready to hit the second serve. He should think about placing the serve in a specific location, or just getting it in play.

SERVING OUT OF BREATH. The server wants to have his breathing under control before taking his serve so he is relaxed. This will help his timing during the subsequent point.

HITTING A BAD TOSS. Bad ball tosses produce bad serves. This wastes an opportunity for a good serve.

Self-coaching is the key to playing smart tennis. The player who practices making adjustments and using reminders will prevent and fix mental and physical errors and be able to compete at a high level of play. He will develop self-coaching techniques for every aspect of his game and will use these techniques throughout every match he plays.

10

How To Compete

A GOOD COMPETITOR HAS AN OVERWHELMING WILL TO WIN. HE HAS tremendous spirit and plays smart tennis whether winning or losing. He stays positive, convinced his skills and his self-coaching techniques will keep him competitive in any match. And he overcomes adversity. Having faced critical situations in the past, he is confident in his ability to succeed.

A good competitor is aware of several essential aspects of competition in every match:

▶▶ He sees every point as an opportunity to compete. His determination to win every point places a burden on his opponent's ability to concentrate.

▶▶ He understands the significance of the score in each game and in each set.

▶▶ He knows how to play the big points. His opponent will have to beat him; he will rarely beat himself on the big points.

The player who competes knows best how to exert and how to handle pressure throughout each match. To be a good competitor, the player must realize that whatever he is doing on the court, there is always an aspect of pressure involved. The greatest pressure will come while he is playing big points, protecting a lead, and serving for the match (or to stay in the match), but the smart competitor will be aware that exerting and handling pressure is continuous in all aspects of match play.

IMPORTANCE OF EVERY POINT

A smart player realizes that *every point, win or lose, is significant.* To be the best competitor possible, he must work for every point and must consider every point important. A player who plays loose points leaves the door open for his opponent; a good competitor wants to close the door. He knows he will be mentally tough and will not suffer from lapses of concentration if he is used to playing to win every point. When things are not going well, he is aware that there is always a chance of coming back until game point itself has been lost. *The bigger the comeback, the greater the psychological edge gained for future points in the match.*

SIGNIFICANCE OF THE SCORE

The player who competes well and wins a high percentage of his matches does so because he understands the significance of the score and its relationship to the outcome of a game or set. *The objective of the player is to make his opponent play from behind.* If this is not possible, then he must try to stay within striking distance. The goal: *Win the first point, take two of the first three points, and be the first player to reach 40.* Ideally, he wants to extend his lead by two points, which creates both a cushion for him, and greater pressure for his opponent.

The first point of a game is a significant point for both players. A good competitor focuses from the outset because he knows *the first point can set the tone for the remainder of the game.* The winner of this point is not only off to a good start, but has succeeded in gaining an edge and putting pressure on his opponent as they go into the next point.

If possible, the player wants to increase his lead and gap in the score to two points, which would take some pressure off him and redirect the pressure toward his opponent. The player with a 30-Love lead has a tremendous advantage, for he now has to win only two of the next four points in any order to win the game.

If he is not able to attain a two-point lead, he still has a goal to win two of the first three points. This will put him up 30-15 and will still give him an edge. He now only has to win one of the next two points to become the first player to reach 40. If the player is first to reach 40, he has the odds in his favor, and his opponent, who is left at 30, now has to win three points in a row…which is very difficult to do.

STAYING WITHIN STRIKING DISTANCE

If the player should fall behind in the game or set, he must remain competitive by staying within striking distance of his opponent. *He needs to stay close in the score at all times throughout the match to keep some pressure on his opponent and to shorten any necessary comeback effort.* A player must stay within one point in a game score to keep in striking distance. Once his opponent gains a two-point edge, he has a cushion and only needs to split every two points to win the game. At Love-15, he needs to win the next point to avoid being down by two points, and to have a chance to win two of the first three points. If the score is Love-30, it is critical for the player to win the next point to keep within striking distance.

A player behind in the game score must battle to prevent his opponent from getting to 40 first. At the very least, he wants to reach 30 by the time his opponent reaches 40. Once his opponent gets to 40, pressure increases considerably, and *luck alone could end the game.* The longer the player can keep his opponent at 30, the more he is able to maintain some breathing room.

A good competitor strives to stay on serve so he will remain within one game in the set score. However, his opponent may break his serve and the player still will be within striking distance. He must fight to avoid a second break, however, which would lead to frustration and take him out of range, especially against a good server. Once a second break occurs, an opponent can play more aggressively because he has a cushion, and his confidence will increase due to his momentum from winning games.

GETTING A FAST START

The first three games of each set are crucial to both players. In the first set, it is important to get off to a good start by holding serve. The player must curb any feelings of nervousness at the outset and play a sound service game that will set a standard for the match. Any remaining nerves should subside once he holds his service game and is on the scoreboard. A good competitor will recognize if his opponent is struggling with nerves, is not warmed up fully, or is having trouble timing the pace, spin, or depth of the serve. These circumstances will help him hold serve. Also, *his opponent's first service game may be the easiest one to break,* especially if he is not putting a high percentage of first serves in play. He might not have a good feel yet for the timing on his serve, volleys, and groundstrokes. Under these conditions, his opponent is likely to make a few unforced errors, and the player must be set to capitalize on his vulnerability.

The player's goal for the set is to win two or three of the first three games, and to be the first to win his fourth and fifth game. Once he has a two-game lead, the player need only split games to run out the set. He wants to get up in the score as soon as possible to force his opponent to play from behind and feel constant pressure to stay in the match.

ADVANTAGE OF THE "UP GAME"

If the player wins the toss, he should elect to serve. The exceptions to this rule would be if he has a weak serve/strong return combination or is too nervous to start serving. Electing to serve gives him the opportunity to gain the psychological advantage of the "up game" in the set score (1-0, 2-1, etc.). This way, his opponent is always playing from behind. Having to do this every service game adds constant pressure and can wear emotionally on him, especially at the end of the set where holding serve becomes more critical and therefore more difficult.

The up game also exerts pressure on his opponent because if he does not hold serve, the break will make the score seem worse than it really is. For example, a set score of 3-0 has a three-game gap that neither looks good nor feels good to his opponent. From the score, it appears that he is getting out of striking distance. However, he can still stay within striking distance if he holds his next service game. If he stays within one service break, he keeps the match close, and it will take only a short comeback to even the score. Ultimately, one of two things will happen: either the player will hold serve, maintain his break, and win the set; or his opponent will make a comeback, and the player will find himself in a very different situation.

PLAYING FROM BEHIND

If the player has fallen behind in the set, he realizes he is entering a critical time once his opponent has won his fourth game. If his opponent also has a service break, he has a significant cushion at this time of the match. This serves as a warning signal that the player needs to dig in and fight harder for every point. Although there is still breathing room, he must not contribute any points to his opponent with unforced or mental errors. Pressure on the player will increase with every new game, and any mistakes will be costly. The burden of catching up and working to stay even with his opponent with the up game adds even more pressure to the player who must fight to stay within striking distance. He must prevent his opponent from winning his fifth game, at which time every game becomes a must game for the losing player.

After his opponent wins his fourth game, the player still has a little cushion; after the fifth, there is none, and even luck can end the game and set. If the player drops serve at 3-4, his opponent will be serving for the set; however, if he drops serve at 4-5, he not only loses the set, but he also allows his opponent to start serving the second set and have the opportunity of the up game.

If he takes the first set, his opponent has quite an advantage. The pressure on him has been reduced because he only has to win one of the next two sets to win the match. At the same time, he has intensified the pressure on the player who has to play from a set behind, and must now win two sets in a row.

CRITICAL NEEDS

The player who is behind must strive for two things by the end of the first set. *First, he wants to be winning more points per game (or trading games, if possible), so he can remain positive and gain confidence in playing more evenly with his opponent.* If he has not been winning many points off his opponent's serve during the first set, he must find a way to become more competitive. That is, if he never gets to 40, or rarely wins more than one or two points off his opponent's serve, then he must determine how he can prevent this domination from continuing. He must focus on the return games, and think of ways to break serve. He must recognize what the server is doing successfully, and make the necessary adjustments on his return of serve. The sooner he can get accustomed to the spins, depth, and speed of his opponent's serve, the sooner he will be capable of winning more points.

The player who is behind must start toward the end of the first set to put a higher percentage of returns in play than he has previously. He still may not win the set, but he will force his opponent to play more balls, exert more physical and mental energy, and possibly commit unforced errors. He will add pressure to his opponent's serve if he is able to return more effectively, and will gain more confidence as he keeps more balls in play. This self-assurance can lead him to become more aggressive in his shots, and ultimately could shift the momentum in his favor.

The second thought the losing player must keep in mind is that he must hold his last service game of the first set, and force his opponent to hold serve to win the set from him. Not only will this make the score closer and give him confidence going into his next service game, but it will place more pressure on his opponent's service game. If the player loses the set, at least he will be able to get off to a better start by serving first and placing himself in a position to have the up game.

TURNING THINGS AROUND

The player who has lost the first set needs to turn things around as quickly as possible to keep the pressure from increasing. *The best way to do this is to get the first service break.* He already has been working to win as many points as possible on his opponent's serve, so he must maintain that pressure by putting a high percentage of service returns in play while he strives to get ahead in the score. Once he forces him to play from behind, there is added pressure on his serve. The server might press a little harder which will tend to throw off his timing on his first serve. It then becomes easier to put the ball in play with a good return off a second serve, and allows the player more opportunities to win points.

If unable to break serve, he must hold serve and keep the score close if he is going to turn the match around. There will be extra pressure on him if he has not been able to reverse things by the time this set reaches the critical stage (when his opponent is first to win his fourth game). The player realizes the dire consequences of having his serve broken and having to play from behind in the second set. His opponent will have less pressure and with this tremendous boost in confidence, he could break the match wide open with a break.

GETTING BACK IN A MATCH

The player who is a good competitor understands that if he can stay within striking distance, there is always the possibility he might get an opportunity to get back in the match. If his opponent considers him to be the better player (even though his opponent is ahead in the match), he might become satisfied with a moral victory rather than a real victory. If this occurs, he might not fight hard enough as the player begins to make his comeback.

It is also possible his opponent might experience a variety of mental changes that would allow the player the chance to get back in the match. The player realizes that at crunch time comes the *moment of truth* for his opponent who might begin playing "not to lose," who might choke, or who might engage in a premature victory celebration if he has been easily winning games. There is also a possibility that the player might decide to go down swinging, and this change in attitude could pull him back into the match. The player who knows how to compete will stay positive and always hope for the opportunity to launch a comeback.

MORAL VICTORY

The opponent who is in a position to win the match might become content with a moral victory instead of a real one. Just being able to stay close with someone he considers to be a much better player, or to go three sets with, is a victory in itself to an opponent who is satisfied with a moral victory. Instead of continuing to fight for the win, he allows the stronger player to win points at a critical time and get back into the match. As this begins to happen, he tends to fold becoming less and less able to resist the player's comeback. This occurs because he is satisfied with the way he has played in the match and believes that he does not necessarily have to win to feel good about his play. *If he subconsciously feels this way, he will find a way to lose the match because he never really believed he could win.* He (or any player like this) will never reach his full potential because he will rarely close out matches with a player he considers to be superior. He can accept losing even though victory is within sight. A good competitor will never possess this attitude.

PLAYING 'NOT TO LOSE'

There is a possibility that at the moment of truth his opponent might decide to become cautious and protect his lead in an attempt to hold on to win the match. He might change from playing aggressively and winning to playing not to lose. He will begin to add too much margin for error into most of his shots, to hit slower shots, and to become less aggressive. This lower level of play allows the player to compete more evenly with him, and gives the player the opportunity to win more points. This could make the difference in a crucial game so that he now has gained some momentum and the match begins to turn around. His opponent has lowered his intensity level such that he has allowed the player to become more competitive. As he gains momentum, the pressure begins to build on his opponent at a time when his intensity is dropping and the player's confidence is increasing. Many matches start to turn around in this way as the opponent is moving in a downward spiral while the player is moving in an upward one. A good competitor realizes that he must stay close, remain patient, and await the opportunity to capitalize on this possible change in his opponent's mental attitude.

CHOKING

An opponent with a lead at the moment of truth also might be gripped by the pressure and succumb to nerves or fear. He internalizes the significance of the moment and may be overcome by pressure and nerves and choke. This will affect the timing of his strokes, and he will be more likely to commit errors and have trouble keeping the ball in play. Whether or not he really has enough confidence to win the match is determined at this time. Even though he may still believe he can win, if he allows the negative emotion of fear to overcome him, his play will begin to deteriorate. He may double fault or miss an easy shot that causes him to lose a critical game.

Everyone feels a certain degree of nervousness from pressure. It is a natural feeling that is hard to escape; however, a good competitor uses effective self-coaching skills to help himself through these times. One of the most effective strategies: Smile to break the tension.

PREMATURE VICTORY CELEBRATION

Another opportunity for the player to get back into the match might occur when his opponent prematurely believes he has won. This could take place when he becomes overconfident with his lead, is winning games easily, and victory appears imminent. One or two more games and the match is his. He begins to think that the match is a foregone conclusion and the next game a mere formality. He is so comfortable with his lead that he begins to relax, lowering his level of concentration. As a result, he plays a few loose points, drops a game, and his cushion is reduced. Meanwhile, the once-trailing player is now back in the match. He is pumped and knows he has a chance to win.

STAYING POSITIVE

In addition to the mental changes that might occur within his opponent, there is an attitude change which the player himself might initiate to turn a match around. He strives to stay positive, and hopes that some of his shots that have been just missing will start going in. However, as his opponent gets closer to victory, the player might begin to believe that he may not be able to win the match. Once his opponent has won his fourth game, the player realizes he has one more possible adjustment to make. He decides to "go down swinging" with more aggressive shots, at the same time changing the tempo of the game. Even if his opponent is playing well, these aggressive shots will force him to adjust his timing and make it more difficult to win points. The player stays positive and finds himself winning points. Suddenly, he feels he is back in the match.

The pressure of wanting to win so badly may have been causing his timing to be off. Once he realizes he might not win, he stops fighting himself. Now, the pressure is off his shots and a reversal becomes possible. His muscles become more relaxed and so his timing improves and his strokes flow more naturally. The player gains confidence and starts to feel the ball better with his more aggressive play. His decision to keep a positive attitude and attempt one last adjustment in his game helps him to compete even when faced with possible defeat.

It is possible the player's attempted comeback may not be successful. His aggressive tactic might cause his shots to become more erratic; but, if he believes he has nothing to lose, then going down swinging is worth a try at that stage in the match. At the very least, he will feel he has given his all and has been defeated by a better opponent that day.

THE FINAL SET

If a player is successful in gaining momentum, then he finds himself in a one-set match. He will have to compete well, for the edge in the third set will go to the better competitor. Again, it is important to remember that the first three games are important for each player in order to get off to a good start. The opponent who won the first set must attempt to get his momentum going again by striving for that first break in the third set. The player who won the second set already has the momentum from having been able to draw even in the match. This has taken some pressure off, and he wants to continue building momentum in the final set by getting the first service break.

It is very important to hold every serve to keep the up game during the third set. The player is aware of the psychological edge and the pressure placed on his opponent who feels he must hold his serve to stay even (or catch up), in this determining set. During the first three games, the player must guard against any feeling of negative relaxation which might have resulted from winning a "come from behind" struggle against his opponent in the second set.

The pressure of crunch time in the third set will be felt by both players if they are on serve, or if each stays within striking distance of one another. If the player is up 4-3, there is still pressure from his opponent who has remained close and could even the score with the next game. There is pressure on the player to remain steady and focused as he is in sight of winning the match.

However, there is more pressure on his opponent who does not have the up-game advantage, and who must prevent the player from winning his fifth game placing his opponent in danger of losing the match. Once one of the players wins his fifth game, or if at 6-all they go to a tiebreak, then all points become critical to both the players. *In a tiebreak, the player wants to make his opponent play from behind.* He must hold all his own service points, and work to split his opponent's service points.

PROTECTING A LEAD

Once he has taken a good lead, such as 4-0 or 5-1, the player must maintain his high intensity to protect it and lessen the likelihood of opening the door for a comeback by his opponent. To retain a high intensity level, he must find a way to challenge himself and to keep focused on winning every point. Two examples of good challenges would be either trying to break his opponent's serve again, or trying to prevent his opponent from winning more games than he did in the previous set. He needs to concentrate on maintaining the pressure on his opponent in order to keep it off himself.

If the player fails to remain in his high intensity level, a smart opponent can take the opportunity to begin his comeback. As his opponent works himself back into the match, fear of losing the lead can enter the player's mind. This is the time when his ability to self-coach and compete are greatly challenged and he must:

1 Focus on the fact that he is still winning and has a cushion—the pressure is still on his opponent.

2 Check that his body language reflects confidence and control.

3 Remind himself to hustle to increase his intensity level.

4 Find a way to stop his opponent's momentum and not let fear dictate his own game.

4 Reduce his unforced errors, avoid short points, and make his opponent work for each point.

5 Treat each point with a big-point mentality (more on this later).

The player's goal is to return to a high intensity level as quickly as possible, and definitely by the time his opponent gets within one game in the score.

Tennis is a game of streaks, and a streak can end at any time. His opponent may relax after drawing even or gaining the lead because he is no longer playing from behind and is feeling less pressure. His relaxation is an opportunity for the player to break the streak. If this is not the case, he will have to have reached high intensity to stop the streak.

PLAYING THE BIG POINTS

In a close match, a good competitor knows that the difference between winning and losing is determined by how well he plays the big points or big games. The big points are break points, set points, tiebreak points, and match points. All points in a critical game—after the player or his opponent has won his fifth game, for instance—are considered big points. These points are the greatest test of a player's ability to utilize his inner coach because it is while preparing for and playing these points that all facets of the mental game need to be realized. A good competitor realizes that the first big points played in a match will affect big points played later.

While playing a big point the player must rely on his best shots to set up the point, and to try to make his opponent beat him with his weakest shot. The smart competitor knows what wins and uses that knowledge during the big points. He recalls which shots have been successful in the match, and he now depends on those shots that have been winning the most points on a consistent basis. And, he knows he must avoid those shots which his opponent has been hurting him with.

A GAME PLAN FOR BIG POINTS

The player must develop a plan for the big points. Consider what might be called the Reverse Golden Rule: *Do unto the opponent what you would not want the opponent to do unto you.* For example, the passing shot is one of the hardest shots to execute under pressure, especially from the weaker side. If the player wants to avoid hitting a passing shot, he must get to the net first and force his opponent to pass him. If the player is serving, he can serve and volley; as the returner, he can chip and charge. In addition, if there is a particular shot in which the player lacks confidence, he should strive to avoid having to hit it using good point development.

SERVING DECISIONS

The player has four decisions to make if he is serving in a big game or for a big point:

    1 He must decide if he wants to serve and volley or stay back. If he chooses to serve and volley, he needs to remind himself to keep the ball in play with a good first volley;

2 He must decide which type of serve he wants to hit: flat, slice, or topspin;

3 He needs to decide the location to which he will serve. Based on earlier experience in the match, he will want to hit the type of serve and to the location that has met with the greatest success thus far. Another possible choice would be to serve into his opponent's body, which could result in a more defensive return and allow for an easier first volley or first shot;

4 He must decide at what speed he wants to hit the serve. This will depend on how well he is serving that day and what speed has given his opponent the most trouble.

SERVING ADVICE

On a crucial point, it is imperative for the player to get his first serve in to put pressure on his opponent. If he has a high percentage of first serves going in and he is feeling very confident, he may choose to hit his flat serve at full speed (especially if he is ahead in the score). However, the smart player knows how difficult it is to win points with second serves against a good opponent, and so he does not want to place extra pressure on his second serve and risk a double fault. For his first serve, he then may choose to hit a spin serve at a faster speed than his normal second serve. This extra speed would make it a more aggressive serve and therefore, more suitable as a first serve. It would also be the same spin the player would use on his slower second serve, if necessary. *Hitting the same spin on both serves makes the transition easier from first to second serve.*

The most conservative approach in a pressure situation would be to use two second serves. Second serves have more margin for error and the player can better compensate for feelings of fatigue and pressure. This serve has a better chance of success, and so he can avoid the pressure of a second serve and a possible double-fault. Although his opponent might have an easier time with the return, he probably will not take the extra risk of going for a winner. This is a crucial point for him also, so he is likely to feel some pressure and play more conservatively to make sure he gets the return in play. Because the second serve is similar to the first, the only adjustment to be made is to vary the trajectory, amount of spin, or speed needed on the second serve to compensate for what was lacking in the first serve.

There is a risk of hitting a flat serve and then a spin serve for the second, especially if a different grip or ball toss location is required. With this situation, there is no transfer of information from the first to the second serve because they are two totally different serves. On the other hand, there would be a good transfer of information if the two serves are of the same type. The spin serve will not be able to be hit as fast as a flat serve, so his opponent will not have to deal with as much speed. However, there is a greater chance that the spin serve will go in, and therefore, the player can avoid the need for a second serve.

On a crucial serve, *the player should take as much time as possible in preparation hopefully making his opponent over-anxious, nervous, or distracted during the wait.* He might lose his edge and his concentration if he is forced to wait a longer time than usual between points. The time between his opponent's last shot and the upcoming one increases during this interval, and this helps to cool him down physically. (A smart returner will back away and try to refocus). The player must be prepared both mentally and physically to hit a good serve. He should remind himself to take a deep breath to help himself relax and to get a good supply of oxygen into his lungs. He executes the same ritual as he would on any other point. As he bounces the ball, he reminds himself to relax his body throughout the service motion for better timing, and begins to focus his eyes on the ball. When he feels relaxed, he should begin his service motion.

SERVING FOR THE MATCH
Serving for the match can be the most difficult service game to hold. However, this task can be made much easier if the player prepares himself properly and applies pressure on his opponent as he serves the preceding game. After winning his fifth game, he might think he doesn't need to win the next game to win the match. He rationalizes that he has been serving well and feels confident he will be able to hold serve. He then tends to coast and not concentrate fully as his opponent serves to stay in the match. This is a huge mental error for several reasons:
- ▶▶ The player is risking lowering his intensity level before his big service game.
- ▶▶ He will help his opponent gain confidence by winning an easy game (which should have been difficult).
- ▶▶ He will be losing a good opportunity to break serve.

The smart player realizes that if he fights hard to break serve, then he will not have to deal with the pressure of serving out the match. *Even if he loses the game, he knows he has prepared properly by maintaining a high intensity level.* Before he begins his service game, he reminds himself how he wants to play this game:

- ▸▸ Get a high percentage of first serves in play
- ▸▸ Commit no unforced errors
- ▸▸ Concentrate on winning the first point
- ▸▸ Stay ahead in the score
- ▸▸ Play all the points with a 'big point' mentality.

Once the game begins, he must stay focused and remind himself to relax before each point.

RETURNING TIPS

There are several thoughts the player must review as the receiver. He must try to anticipate which serve his opponent will attempt. *If there has been a particular serve with which he has been beating him consistently that day, it is most probable that this is the serve the player will see.* The fact that he is mentally prepared for a serve increases his chances of making a successful shot.

The player must remind himself to hit a return that would be effective regardless if his opponent serves and volleys, or stays on the baseline. He should plan which shot he should hit if the serve comes to his forehand or his backhand. The player might visualize hitting the ball to a specific target, even take a practice swing.

Before assuming the ready position, the player should take a deep breath to help relax his body. *He should be prepared before the server is to demonstrate his readiness for the challenge and his eagerness to get the point started.* In doing so, he gives himself a positive message and it is possible that his opponent might feel some tension as he recognizes the player's confident attitude. This could be just enough to throw off his opponent's timing on his serve and force a second serve, giving the player an advantage.

As the server steps to the baseline, *the player should start moving his feet or body, which stimulates the brain and signals his readiness.* He must remind himself to focus on his opponent's ball toss to see if he can determine which serve will be coming. He must watch the ball, listen to its sound at contact, and then read the direction the ball is going together with the speed at which it is traveling to know what body and racquet preparation will be necessary.

If his opponent misses his first serve, the player should give himself two reminders before the second serve: Remember to take a step forward to compensate for a slower serve, and remind himself to step in to the shot. These reminders and his movement stimulate the brain and help the player stay focused for his return. Finally, he must decide if he intends to chip and charge if he gets a serve on which he typically likes to come in. The player now is prepared both mentally and physically for the return, and his chances for success have increased.

The true competitor learns through experience to compete well, and stays positive in any situation. He reminds himself to make use of all that he has learned on the practice court and in past competitions. He rarely beats himself in a match. By getting in the habit of competing for each and every point; winning the first point of each game; and practicing to keep the score close, he will become a higher-level competitor.

11

Getting in the Flow

THERE IS A NATURAL FLOW TO EVERY MATCH. THE SMART PLAYER WILL use everything he has mastered up to this point—his mental toughness, self-coaching ability, and his understanding of percentage tennis, point development, patterns of play, and tactics—to influence the flow of his matches. He will keep five things in mind that will positively or negatively affect that flow:

▸▸ Understanding the streaks in a match
▸▸ Avoiding mental lapses
▸▸ Controlling the tempo between points
▸▸ Knowing how to build momentum
▸▸ Developing a second wind.

POSITIVE AND NEGATIVE STREAKS

Tennis is a game of streaks. To prepare mentally for each game, a player must use his self-coaching skills to identify those streaks, and to analyze what is happening in a match. The two major streaks that are significant to the outcome of a match happen on a player's service games, and on his return-of-service games. Each of these streaks has a positive and negative side.

The positive side of a serving streak begins when the player holds his serve. Once he is able to hold his serve consistently, he has established it as a weapon in the match, and has gained the confidence to rely on his serve in crucial situations. When he drops his serve a negative streak begins.

The same happens on service returns. A player who breaks his opponent's serve begins a positive streak and gives him the confidence that he can break him again. A negative streak starts when a player fails to break his serve.

A player has to be able to begin and sustain one of his positive streaks to stay competitive in the set. Whether he holds serve consistently and fails to break his opponent's serve, or whether he breaks serve consistently and fails to hold his own serve is not important to the final outcome. *What is crucial is who breaks his negative streak first*, for that player gains not only the lead in the set, but also gains a psychological edge in the match.

STARTING A POSITIVE STREAK

Be on the lookout for good opportunities to start positive streaks. *The easiest way to hold serve is when the player wins at least one or two points from his serve alone.* He can serve an ace, force a return error, or force a weak return that sets up a finish shot. All these points are credited to the serve. He then has only to win the remaining two or three points using his other strokes. This is a much easier task than having to win all his points in the game that way because it is very difficult to do against an opponent in high intensity.

The best opportunity to break serve is when his opponent:

▸▸ fails to put a high percentage of first serves in play
▸▸ gives away a free point by committing an unforced or mental error
▸▸ misses an easy shot
▸▸ serves a double fault.

Breaking serve is easier to do when a player has to win only three or fewer points. The smart player recognizes opportunities and knows he may not get very many. Before his opponent serves he uses a reminder, "Put the return in play," to take advantage of every situation and make his opponent pay for his errors. He knows that *a service break is an important event in a match, and that it becomes even more significant if it is followed by holding serve.*

If the player is unable to break serve, he still wants his opponent to play a long game and work hard to hold his serve. This puts him in a better position to win the game, but also *forces his opponent to struggle so hard to hold serve that he then finds it more difficult to devote all his energy toward breaking serve in the next game.* It will also make him anxious about his capability to hold serve. The player wants to hold serve as easily as possible in order to devote more energy toward breaking his opponent's serve. This combination of holding serve with ease and forcing him to struggle to hold serve will wear him out emotionally and can lead to frustration and errors.

Two big servers playing against each other will have a difficult time breaking one another. One service break may be all that is needed to win a set, or a set might be determined by which player performs better in the tiebreak. Good baseline players generally have average serves and excellent service returns. Therefore, they may be able to break serve more easily than they can hold serve. In order to stay competitive in a match, a player must be able to dominate in at least one area. *A champion dominates at both ends.*

BREAKING A NEGATIVE STREAK

Every player needs to know how to break a negative streak. The most effective method is comparable to the one a smart player uses to build momentum.

▸▸ Start by playing more evenly and then winning more points, gradually chipping away at his advantage. The player must get as close as possible to winning the game, so that the next opportunity he has to break the negative streak, he will have the confidence to do so.

▸▸ The player might also add more hustle, and try to look for the "little positives" in the match as a way to gain some momentum (more later in this chapter).

▸▸ The player must remind himself to try different placements or more aggressive shots. If he is struggling to hold serve, he must focus on getting a higher percentage of first serves in play, even if he has to hit the serve at three-quarters' speed.

▸▸ The player should consider hitting his second serve more aggressively to set up the point; he might double-fault, but since he was losing his serve anyway, he has little to lose in being more aggressive.

▸▸ He must remind himself to make his opponent play from behind. This could be the reason the streak is occurring—his opponent has never had to play from behind during that streak.

UNDERSTANDING ENVIRONMENTAL FACTORS

The sun and the wind can affect the outcome of matches, and a smart player will use self-coaching techniques to utilize those factors to his advantage. On a sunny day, it is important for him to hold serve when he isn't looking into the sun, and focus on breaking serve when his opponent is serving into the sun. If he can do that consistently, he only has to win one other game to take the set.

Wind gusts can affect the flow of a match. Usually, it is easier for a player to win games when the wind is at his back rather than when he is hitting into it. For that reason, he should focus on holding serve when serving with the wind, and trying to break serve when his opponent is serving into the wind. Obviously, he wants to win every game on both sides; however, the wind makes his task more difficult because it is unlikely he will be able to establish his normal game.

A reminder: In windy conditions focus on keeping the ball in play. It's okay to win ugly. Reminders are particularly helpful on windy days because the player must make continuous adjustments. Two good reminders for playing in windy conditions are:

- ▸▸ Hit passing shots and lobs with less clearance over the net when hitting with the wind.
- ▸▸ Against the wind, use slice shots often. They stay low, and the wind will slow down the ball even more, making shots difficult to reach before they bounce a second time.

OVERCOMING MENTAL LAPSES

Most players will lose concentration at some point in the match. A smart player will recognize the signs of a mental lapse and will provide himself reminders to concentrate and focus on subsequent points.

There are two types of mental lapses in which the player experiences a loss in concentration: letdowns and negative relaxations. Letdowns occur after negative results. Negative relaxations occur after positive results. Both produce unfavorable outcomes and must be avoided. The smart player is aware of situations when either lapse might take place, and he uses reminders to prevent them.

LETDOWNS

Letdowns are likely to occur after the player has failed to capitalize on a good opportunity. He realizes he might not get many such chances during the match, and he is disappointed by his inability to take advantage of the situation. He is aware also that his opponent will gain confidence if he continuously is unable to take advantage of these circumstances. Some examples of lost opportunities include:

- ▸▸ having break points and not breaking serve
- ▸▸ missing easy shots
- ▸▸ not winning a game in which an opponent double-faults

➤ blowing a 40-Love lead

➤ serving for the set and losing the game

➤ losing the set in a tiebreak.

A letdown is a natural response after any of these disappointments. If a player lets down too often in a match, he jeopardizes his chances of making a comeback or getting off to a good start in a new game. Smart players avoid letdowns by challenging themselves to win the next point or game following a letdown, and by having a plan to accomplish this.

NEGATIVE RELAXATION

Negative relaxation is a mental lapse in concentration triggered by success. It occurs when a player feels comfortable with his lead and relaxes too much. It happens in these kinds of situations:

➤ At 40-Love

➤ Being up 4-0 or 5-0 in a set

➤ After breaking serve or winning a set.

These are positive situations that the smart player wants to convert into positive streaks. He does not want to allow his opponent a chance to get back into the match. He knows he has the momentum and he wants to keep it as long as possible. He wants his opponent to work hard every point, and he needs to avoid playing loose shots on his end.

CONTROLLING TEMPO BETWEEN POINTS

A smart player plays at his own tempo, not his opponent's. Under the rules of tennis, players are permitted to take only twenty-five seconds between points. How much time he takes depends on his physical condition and the score in the match. *The general rule is to slow down and take the maximum time allowed between points when losing or when an opponent has the momentum.* There are two reasons for this:

1 The player will have more time to analyze the situation and to plan the proper adjustments.

2 Slowing down play might force an opponent to lose concentration or patience.

Taking time between points can reverse an opponent's momentum. The player who does not take the maximum time allows his opponent to continue dictating the tempo and controlling the match.

There are several specific occasions when the player should take *more* time between points than he ordinarily does:

▸▸ When he feels fatigued, he should take additional time to recuperate.

▸▸ When he is serving and is down in the game score, he needs time to decide how he wants to play the next point. This can give an opponent time to become nervous or lose concentration.

▸▸ When the player is disappointed by his play, additional time guards against a letdown.

▸▸ Before a big point, he should take extra time to plan his strategy, whether he is ahead or behind in the score.

WHEN TO SPEED UP PLAY

Players should take less time between points when they are winning to continue their momentum and to maintain their concentration. They also don't want to give their opponents sufficient time to plan adjustments. *Players with momentum want to win as many points and games in as short a length of time as possible.*

There are two specific situations when the player should get the next point started quickly:

1 When his opponent is visibly upset with himself, such as after committing a mental error. He wants him to be thinking about the last point, taking away his time to prepare mentally for the upcoming point.

2 When the player has won a quick point. The only exception is if he is behind in that game. If this is the situation, he should take extra time to plan the next point carefully.

THE 'LITTLE POSITIVES'

One of the ways the player can start to build momentum is by looking for the "little positives" in the match. Little positives include anything favorable that makes the player feel as if he is playing better and more evenly with his opponent. He should analyze his game to determine if he is starting to do something, either offensively or defensively, that he has not been able to do up to this point. Some of these little positives he should look for include:

▸▸ Hitting more shots per point

▸▸ Keeping more set-up shots in play

▸▸ Starting to make passing shots

▸▸ Getting more first serves in play and winning points on serve

▸▸ Hitting sharper volleys

▸▸ Hustling to get to more balls and playing better defense. *A player can use his defensive skills to help jump-start his offense.*

The player should also analyze the play of his opponent and try to get little positives from things his opponent might have stopped doing well. Examples include:

▸▸ Double faulting or missing a high percentage of first serves

▸▸ Making more unforced errors

▸▸ Playing less aggressively

▸▸ Having emotional outbursts.

The player should feed off each of these positives as they occur, and continue to pump himself up through reminders such as "that's better" or "way to play." As the little positives accumulate, he will feel the momentum of the match begin to turn in his favor. His confidence will increase as his feelings of pressure and tension decrease.

The most helpful of the little positives is *keeping the ball in play more* in order to have longer points. Hitting more shots per point will force the player to raise his intensity level because he will have to concentrate more and cut down on unforced errors. If he keeps the ball in play longer than he had been, he will start winning more points and will be playing more evenly with his opponent. Once he wins two games in a row he has the momentum. The smart player will use this system of building momentum to jump-start his game, and raise his chances for a comeback and win matches that seemed in doubt.

DEVELOPING A SECOND WIND

Often there comes a point late in a match when it becomes a battle of endurance. Both the player and his opponent are struggling physically and mentally to continue playing at a high level. Exhausted, they question whether or not they will be able to finish the match. This might occur early in the third set, so some difficult games are still ahead. The smart player knows he can get his second wind if he can fight hard enough to get ahead in the score, possibly by getting the first service break. This breakthrough decreases the burden of fatigue and will help him regain his strength with an increase in adrenalin. This will enable him to start playing at a higher intensity level, which in turn will allow him to dominate his still-fatigued opponent. The smart player understands that a losing player never gains his second wind and that is why he is so determined and fights so hard to be the first to get ahead.

Understanding the natural flow of every match gives the smart player an edge in competition. If he is aware of the streaks in a match, avoids mental lapses, learns how to control the tempo between points, and knows how to build momentum and to find his second wind, he will become a very strong competitor. On court, the smart player will use everything he has mastered in the mental game. He will bring his *Inner Coach* to each match.

Epilogue

SOME DAYS, HOWEVER, NO MATTER WHAT YOU TRY, YOU JUST WON'T BE ABLE to compete at your highest level. Like any player, I have experienced my share of those days. In fact, I would say that over my competitive career, I only played up to my potential five times. And thanks to opponents like Arthur Ashe, I didn't win all of them!

Your goal should be to develop such a well-rounded game that you can win most of your matches with far less than your full potential on display. That requires enormous *concentration and patience.* You have to carefully evaluate your own strengths and weaknesses before and during a match, and adjust constantly to overcome problems. And you can't just be a student of your own game: You have to study your opponent from the moment you walk on the court, tracking his shots and his body language to pick up clues about his weaknesses and strengths. Focusing that hard on the mental side of tennis takes a lot of energy, but smart players know that their mental concentration is often what provides the edge on court.

But the most important thing you can do as a player is to learn the value of persistence. Years ago my dad gave me some great advice: Do at least one thing every day toward reaching your goals. I know that might sound like simple advice, but it served me well during my playing days. The only way you can hone the physical and mental skills to become a champion is by practicing, or doing strength training or cross training a little bit every day—and staying focused on your goal of becoming the best player you can be. With a healthy dose of hard work, a tenacious eye toward improving, and a belief in yourself, any player can overcome on-court weaknesses. I proved it—and you can, too.

ABOUT THE AUTHOR

A native of Evanston, Ill., Dave won two state high school singles championships and helped lead his school to three team titles. He was a two-time All-American at Indiana University and was a member of the U.S. Junior Davis Cup Squad. He played in five Grand Slam tournaments, reaching the third round in singles at Forest Hills and the semifinals in doubles at the Australian Nationals (now the U.S. and Australian Opens).

As a teaching professional, Dave developed a self-coaching system that has helped thousands of players improve their mental toughness on the court. Over a 40-year career, he coached and was instrumental in four players winning national titles, worked with two players who reached the Top 50 in the world on the pro tour, and helped more than 50 students earn college scholarships.

A USPTA Master Professional and member of his high-school and college athletic Halls of Fame, Dave is currently a partner in the Windward Lake Club in Alpharetta, Ga. He lives in Atlanta with his wife Eileen, and has four children and one grandchild.

Printed in the United States
129988LV00003B/2/A